To Paul
stay strong, stay!
Love
L?

C000246193

Take Your Marks, Get Set...

Athletics, Covid, Cancer and Coping!!

Linda Sole

Grosvenor House
Publishing Limited

This book is published by
Grosvenor House Publishing Ltd
Link House
140 The Broadway, Tolworth, Surrey, KT6 7HT.
www.grosvenorhousepublishing.co.uk

A CIP record for this book
is available from the British Library

ISBN 978-1-83975-687-0

Dedicated to Tim

My rock, my soulmate!

Always there when needed, always on
hand with advise and hugs.

This journey could not have happened without the love,
care and support that was given freely and with
dedication and understanding.

No one could wish for more.

Thank you Tim!

Contents

Preface

Hello there!!! Firstly, I would like to thank you from the bottom of my heart for joining me on my journey.

As things unfold, you will see it's not a voyage anyone would want to take, but hopefully by sharing my experiences, I can live in the hope that it may help someone else in the future deal with very unexpected situations that may have to be faced, being that of going through certain circumstances themselves, or being the partner, friend, family or carer for someone in the same position I found myself in.

I have tried for the best part to give you an insight into happenings, and to be open and honest at all times.

During my journey there are some happy and sad, up and down and quite frankly bizarre moments, but all put together they can hopefully make one stronger and more determined to get through whatever lies ahead as best as possible.

I hope you don't mind but I will start the journey with an outline of my life, so as to give you an insight into the way things were before events occurred that would change my life forever. So, settle down and let the journey begin!!

Introduction

It was a very cold February morning in 2020 and as usual we were up very early and off to the South of England Masters Athletics Championships held at Lee Valley Indoor athletics track in North London.

Masters athletics is designed for the more mature athletes, with the age groups starting at 35 years old and go up in five year increments. You only compete in your 5 year age bracket, making it fair for everyone. My age group was 55-59.

It was a journey we had made several times, and we knew it would take about two and a half hours to reach the venue. I had trained well for the championships, and had pushed hard for the 200 metres, a distance I had not done in a major competition before, but I felt that I could manage.

We arrived early as usual, but better to be early than late! Other Athletes started to arrive, and the atmosphere and excitement was building.

Today I had entered the 60 metres and the long jump which were scheduled for the morning and the 200 metres in the afternoon, giving me plenty of time to prepare for it.

The 60 metres was first, and the race went well, and I almost achieved a personal best time. In the long jump I managed to collect a Silver medal, just missing out on the

Gold. I now had a break before the 200 metres in the afternoon, so took some food on-board and re-hydrated.

The time had come to warm up for the event, and I must admit I was feeling very anxious about the race. I had really trained hard for this one and didn't want anything to go wrong. During the warm up for the 200 metres I felt a little tired, and my breathing wasn't as good as I was happy with, but I put it down to just being anxious. We were called to the 'call room' where they hold you before your race. There were quite a few other 200 metre races before mine, so the wait seemed to go on forever. My anxiety was rising to the point I wasn't so sure I could do it. My time came, and we were called to the start line. Again, I didn't seem to feel right, and felt a little 'out of it' but again I put that down to nerves and anxiety. We were called to the blocks, and the starter took his position. "Take your marks, set" and bang, we were off. The first half of the race went really well, but then to my shock and horror I lost all my energy and was flagging badly. In Athletics terms they call it 'hitting the wall' and boy I didn't just hit it, I crashed into it!! I couldn't pick myself up, and despite the cheering from other Athletes I felt weaker and weaker. Something was very wrong. I managed to cross the line in less than a respectable time and felt very ill, almost collapsing on the track. I managed to crawl off the track and found a safe place to lie down as I felt very weak to the point I thought I was going to faint. I don't think anyone saw me, so I raised my legs and done some very deep breathing. The faint feeling passed, and I managed to get back to the call room and collect my things. The journey home was interesting as we always talk about what went well, what didn't go so well, and what could be done better next time. We put the problem with the 200 metres down to over training for it and getting far too anxious about the race. Needless to say, we both could not have been more wrong........................

Chapter 1

Take your marks.

THE EARLY YEARS.

"Take your marks". The starter's words echoed around in my head, butterflies doing dances in my tummy, and feeling slightly sick. In my mind I was as prepared for this race as much as I was ever going to be. I felt good and it was going to be great. His words boomed around in my head again as he said "Get set". I was primed and ready to go. I could feel my heart beating out of my chest in anticipation, ready to burst. Out of the corner of my eye I could see my other competitors and wondered if they were feeling as tense as I was. I thought to myself "I've got this". Time seemed to stand still, but all too quickly the starter shouted "Go". And we were off!!! I was running faster than I had ever ran before. I knew in my mind I was capable of beating the others. I just had to prove it. Time again stood still as I felt myself trip, my arms and legs flailing and thinking to myself this can't be happening. I was only 30 metres into the race. So there you have it. I had stumbled, hit the deck and was now collapsed in a heap on the track watching the others running away from me towards the finish line. I sat there on the track, broken, disappointed and my pride was destroyed. I was crying my eyes out for my Mum. Well that's what you do when your only 8 years old isn't it??

I came into this world on January 30th 1961, a healthy 8lb 8oz baby Girl born to 2 loving parents. I was the eldest of 3 children, having a younger Brother and Sister. Our parents were not well to do, although they both worked really hard, and things were often basic and possibly a little tight financially, but we never went without anything

2

and we knew we were loved. Growing up was a challenge, as it is to most children. We moved to a new house on several occasions and always lived in Council houses, until the government in their wisdom decided to sell them to the tenants. Needless to say, my parents jumped at the chance to own their own home and who could blame them!!!! I changed schools several times, but I never found it hard to make friends. We were free to play outside, climb trees, play in the park, which at the time was called the 'Wreck', though I have no idea why, and go Apple and Plum scrumping and do the things that children should do. Guaranteed I would always get caught which seemed to be a trait that would be with me for years.

My first day at school at the age of 5 was very interesting. We only lived up the road from the school, a 2-3 minute walk. My Mum 'toddled' me off to school with pride in my brand new uniform; hair done in cute little bunches decorated with ribbons, and a yummy lunchbox. I waved my Mum goodbye, and entered the school. I decided very quickly that I didn't like it, and this was not for me so I toddled myself off home, only to be marched back to school by a very irate Mother, and I decided for my best interests and well-being it would be a good idea to stay.

Over time I settled into the various schools I attended and always found that I had a lovely circle of friends. Eventually I developed a strong interest in music and running, which at the time was what we called it. As I have stated, my first running race ended in disaster as I fell over and DNF (Did Not Finish).

At one of the schools I was a pupil at, the nativity play was my chance to shine, and I really wanted to play Mary the leading roll. Sadly, the part went to the daughter of one of the teacher's, which I thought was a little unfair, and I ended up as the Angel Gabriel, a part of some esteem, but I really wanted to be Mary!!!

On a separate occasion, I did win an award for playing the Piano!! I had only received a few lessons, but as I was the only one that could play a little, I won!! 'Gotta be in it to win it'. The only thing was, I had to perform a piece of music to the whole of the school. It was a bit embarrassing as it was very plonky and basic, but at least I did it, and done it with pride.

At the age of 11 I sat what was then the called the 11+. I had worked hard over the years, but had no expectations of passing and secretly I don't think my parents did either, (though why this should have been I have no idea). Anyway, imagine the shock my parents, and myself, had when the results came through and I had passed!!!!! I was in shock, as were my parents, and I still to this day can't work out if they were pleased or not (although secretly I think they were very proud) or a little anxious about the financial implications. A grammar school was going to be a lot more expensive than a comprehensive school, but in my heart of hearts I knew they would do everything to make it work.

THE GROWING UP YEARS.

So off I went to Grammar school with high expectations. Sadly most of my friends had not passed the 11+ and had gone to the local comprehensive school. I so wished I could have gone with them as I knew I would miss them but I would now have to start to make new friends again. All the other pupils were from either well to do or high-flying families and it was obvious I was going to find it a challenge to fit in. But I do like a challenge. I was almost the same height at the age of 11 as I am today, and everyone else seemed so much smaller. My puberty was very advanced for my years, and I actually had breasts, albeit small ones and had started my periods at the age of nine and a half. I did manage to make quite a few new friends, but there was a group of girls who found it hilarious to pick on me, probably because of my height and background. I decided very early on just to ignore them and knuckle down into my new school.

My height advantage paid off in dividends as I was picked for the school netball team as the shooter, the main goal scorer. I was good at scoring goals, and we won most of our games. The other girls seemed to get bored with picking on me, and the problem went away. I settled happily into what was going to be long hard 5 years of schooling.

I remember a time, New Year's Eve I think, when I knew my parents were out and I was left in charge at home. I decided to have a party' and invited friends from school. Wanting to make some sandwiches, the only thing we had was cat food. So, the sandwiches were made. I told everyone it was a specially imported fish paste my Mum had managed to get from France!!! It did make me giggle when everyone seemed to enjoy them, although I did feel a little mean. I kept that little secret to myself. As everyone had bought some alcohol with them, we all got drunk, and one of my friends pissed on my brothers' bed!!! He was not impressed and was very angry. He phoned Mum and Dad at the club they were at and boy did I get it when they got home. I never had any more parties!!!

I was not very good academically, although I tried really hard, but I tended to get bored very quickly and lost interest in most subjects. However, I did excel in sport and had a soft spot for music, appearing in several school musicals, again never getting the lead role but always achieving the second-best role. I was comfortable with this by now. I was caught one day just plonking on the piano when I thought no-one was around. Needless to say, I got busted but to my surprise the school decided to fund piano lessons for me. Sad thing about this was I was taught in a small cupboard with a very creepy piano teacher and decided this was so not for me.

The music side went out of the window when I was shouted at by the teacher to make my "choices" in the third year of schooling for moving forward to GCE examinations. We had to make these decisions to determine which subjects would be best to secure our futures, but I felt I was being pressured into it as I wasn't sure what I wanted to do with my life once I left school. As she was actually the music teacher, I thought I was being clever not choosing music to get back at her. My bad!

However, sport I was good at. I mainly excelled in athletics and was the school champion in Long Jump and sprints and also competed in many inter schools competitions gaining valuable points for our team. I even managed to be school champion at badminton two years running, and also became the local pentathlon champion! I loved my athletics and at every chance I had I was out training, mainly on long jump. Training was not like it is today, with high tech equipment and professional Coaches; it was very basic and could be very painful at times. At the beginning of every athletics season, I would train so hard from the start that most times I could not walk for several days. But that was just the way we done things then, 'back in the day'. Nothing ever came of it, and I left school with no qualifications, and left athletics behind.

Going into what I called the 'Big World' was a bit of a shock to the system as school really doesn't prepare you for what's outside at all, and you have to grow up pretty fast!!! Going into a proper working environment is a bit mind blowing and very scary. All of a sudden little people become big people, and ones to be respected and not just have a laugh and mess about with. The academicals of teachings are great when you're at school, but depending on what sort of career you partake in can become all but useless. Those that go on to do what I call high flying jobs would find the school curriculum useful, but for me, I dropped out of school at the first opportunity and into several factory jobs. Employment was high back in those days, and you could leave a job on a Friday and start a new one on the Monday. How times change?

It was so nice to be earning my own money, and Mum and Dad were good at not taking too much for rent and food. However, they could have done but for some reason didn't. Friday's were the highlight of the week being pay day, and we were given cash weekly, so it was always straight off down the town to buy clothes and records, and then get ready for wild weekends out. Friday and Saturday nights were great!!! Drinking, Discoing, and throwing up when I got home!!!!! I loved the weekends as it made the boring factory jobs worthwhile having something to look forward too. Looking back now in hindsight, I probably could have used my time more wisely, but I was young and having fun.

I did manage to hold down several relationships, some good, some bad, and some just down right ridiculous, but I never seemed to find "the right one". I tried the marriage thing once, a commitment that a lot of people were shocked I made, but sadly it didn't work out and an amicable divorce ensued. I guess I just wasn't very good at the relationship thing, and felt it was a bit overrated!!!!

THE QUITE FRANKLY BIZARRE YEARS.

It was at this point Tim came into my life. We seemed to hit it off straight away, and we both had a very strong interest in music, which caught my attention straight away!!! As I could sing and he could play the guitar, we decided to try and form a band!!! We dropped everything and bolted headlong into being the next best thing since sliced bread. Well that met with much disapproval from almost everyone, with them all saying "You can't do that!!! Get proper jobs!!" Not ones to be told what to do we charged ahead anyway. We pulled in a bass player and drummer and managed to secure a number of 'gigs' at our local Working Men's Clubs. We were going to be great and take on the World!!! Unfortunately we managed to clear the room on our first gig as we were far too loud.

Consequently, all bookings we had at the venue were cancelled and as word filtered out so were all our bookings at the other nearby clubs as well.

Fortunately were thrown a lifeline when an agent was pulling his hair out for a Duo. We explained to him that there would only be one vocal and one guitar, but he was so desperate that he said yes. The work wasn't great, but it paid well and gave us an insight in how to move forward. We had our feet on the first rung of the ladder. Tim took singing lessons, and I bought a piano keyboard which I had to learn to master very quickly as it had amazing drums and backing accompaniment. 'Aquarius Duo' was let loose on the World.

Things went from strength to strength and we became very good. We travelled all over northern Europe, and completed several tours of the UK, including the North East club circuit. Now coming from the South, and only being used to small venues, we were stunned at the size of some of the places. If they like you, you're fine, if they don't you're stuffed!! You also must contend with the Bingo!!! I still don't know to this day how we got away with it, but we did. We managed to blow our equipment up on several occasions but the agency we used were brilliant and lent us a PA system which was bigger and better than what we had been using. We completed several tours successfully. We also deviated a little and took a few summer seasons as Entertainments Managers as well as doubling up as the resident Duo. This proved to be a challenge as one minute you're seeing in top named acts and then running back to your equipment to play to the audience. Also, on several occasions we had to join in with the entertainments team to entertain the kids. It was all fun but 'bloody' hard work. Also on the holiday parks there's a lot of shenanigans that go on, (I think you may guess what they were so I will leave that one there!!!) But that's a whole new book!!!! The saying in the music industry is its all sex drugs and rock and roll. We played some rock and roll but that was about as far as that went!!

One of the worst jobs we took was in the North of Norway, five hundred miles inside the Arctic Circle.

It was our first job abroad, and we were so excited to be offered it we signed the contract without doing any research into where it was!! Only after the paperwork had come through, we checked where the venue was and thought "Oops". But we had signed and now had to go.

We had to drive to Aberdeen, get the ferry to Stavanger and then had a 4-day drive to reach the Hotel. It was in the middle of no-where, it was November, and had 22 hours a day darkness. We were also in trouble as we didn't declare to customs at Stavanger as they were shut. There was no-one there, so we just drove to the venue. The local police were very kind and decided we could stay, but I wish in a way they had sent us home!! The 'gig' didn't work out, so mutually the manager and ourselves decided to call it a day. We were to go to an Agent in Oslo so he could help us. Someone suggested the best way to get there was to drive upwards and then down into Sweden as the roads were better. What they failed to tell us we would need to go over a 5,000-foot glacier/mountain. So, there we were, caught in a snow blizzard, on a 5,000-foot mountain with no heater in the car. At this point Tim decided it would be a good idea to put the snow chains on. He left the car, put on the chains and then returned to the car. His face was blue and I panicked and screamed at him to get us out of the blizzard. We were doing well, albeit slowly, when Tim spotted some dim lights down a ditch on the side of the road. He decided to stop and have a look, much to my indignant screaming of disapproval, and he discovered a car had swerved of the road and was stuck. He pulled the car out, again with me screaming at him to just leave it. The family inside of the car could not have been more grateful, and boy did I feel guilty!! They informed us that it was not uncommon for people to die in their situation which made me feel worse. I must admit that in the end I was glad we had helped them. We made it to Oslo, stayed a week and then returned to the UK via Denmark and Germany.

We were both so glad to be home. The agent who had sent us to Norway apologised profusely and gave us a six-month contract on the Island of Jersey. Now that was more like it!!

For a few years I had been suffering with abnormal periods which were really starting to impact on my life and work, sometimes almost leaving me unable to entertain, being in a lot of pain and having to rush off stage at most inconvenient moments. It was becoming unbearable so I decided to get it checked out and to my horror I was told I had abnormal cells and would need a full hysterectomy. So at that age of 27 it was done. I have to admit, it was one of the best things for me at the time and I have never looked back since. You have to listen to your own body and I would say to anyone most emphatically if you think that you may have a problem get it checked out straight away. It may save your life one day.

Although travelling was fun, it could be very tiring, and we sometimes wondered whether Agents actually looked at maps. We could be entertaining at one venue one night, and then have to travel over 100 miles to the next 'gig'. We always had to take into account we would not finish performing till late, and then have to pack away the equipment which sometimes left little time to sleep and prepare for the next journey and performance. This made it harder living out of a suitcase as it seemed we were always packing and unpacking, and as we would always strive to maintain an extremely high standard of entertainment, it was becoming harder. So after 18 years of being on the road, we decided to settle at home and pick up work in local Clubs and Hotels. We knew there would be enough work as being a seaside resort there were plenty of Hotels and Clubs crying out for good acts. And boy did we get plenty of work, sometimes picking up two venues in one day. But at least the travelling was more manageable, and no suitcases!!!!

Whilst we had been on the road, and on the rare occasions we had some time off, mainly in between summer and winter tours, we always stayed with Mum and Dad when we came home. We never thought about getting our own place as it really didn't seem worth it, and for some reason they always seemed more than happy to have us home, although I can't help thinking sometimes we were a pain in the 'butt'. Even during our time off, we managed to pick up some local 'gigs' which were also good for them as well because they would get lots of nights out, and they really seemed to enjoy themselves and were so supportive. When we were travelling, they would also come on holiday to a lot of the venues we were playing at and Mum even started to sing on Karaoke, and I must admit she wasn't half bad. Dads used to supply the drinks bless him.

Now that we had come off the road and settled into local gigging, we talked about at last getting our own place, and managed to find a small flat locally. We were really worried about telling Mum and Dad as we didn't want to upset them, as they seemed quite comfortable with the situation. We could not have been more wrong!!! We sat them down and broke it to them gently. Mum got all excited and said "Brilliant!! You can have all the furniture and I get to replace it with brand new items!!!" So, we had a flat full of furniture and a very happy Mum.

Dad on the other hand was not so impressed. Not because we were leaving, but because he would have to pay for the new decor in the house!!!!!

THE NORMAL YEARS??

After we had been home for a while, and settled into the flat, I decided that it was time for me to call it a day. I didn't have the heart for the music scene anymore, and things were changing within the industry and I must say not for the better. Well at least not for us. Technology was taking over, and we were having trouble keeping up. We were what I would call good old fashioned entertainers, wanting to make people dance, laugh, and sing and not ones for all the high tech music that was being branded about. We knew it was the right way to move forward, but it was not for us.

To be honest I just wanted to lead a normal life and do a normal job. It was a difficult decision as I didn't want to let Tim down, but for my well-being and sanity I knew it was the right thing to do.

Tim fully understood and carried on for a while on his own, but he decided to give up eventually. We both settled into what was called normal jobs. I took a job at a local well know DIY store followed by my dream job working as a Receptionist at a local Veterinary Practice, a job I still hold down some 17 years on. Tim found employment in Security and built up a very high profile over the years, before becoming a Health and Safety Manager within a well-established College Group environment.

We had a lot of very good years in entertainment, experiencing things most people could only dream of. We were lucky and blessed to have had the chance to do something different. A lot of people even to this day ask me if I miss it, and I can emphatically say No!!!

Just on a sad note, we lost Mum to cancer in 2010. She fought a long hard battle for four and a half years; always maintaining a positive attitude, which I think helped her to fight for so long. She even managed to record herself singing the well-known Vera Lynn song 'we'll meet again' to be played at her funeral. That was the amazing woman she was, and very sadly missed by all who knew her.

In another moment of pure madness, at the age of 35 I bought a Horse. We called him 'The Boy'.

Now I could ride a little but had no idea how to look after a Horse!!! The poor thing had been neglected so he was a little sad. He was only 4 years old when we bought him, and I didn't realise that it was very young for a Horse. He looked at me, I looked at him, and I swear at the same time we both thought "what the hell are we going to do now". I didn't have a clue what we were doing, and it seemed neither did he, which probably wasn't a bad thing as I must admit he was a bit of a bugger, but I thought that was just normal. As usual I was wrong. He was just taking the 'mickey' out of me, much to a lot of people's amusement.

I decided it would be a good idea to call in a riding instructor to help and it proved to be good move. She was very knowledgeable and helped me a lot with the basics before deciding I was ready to partake in some show jumping as this was her main activity to teach. The jumps were assembled in the middle of the school. I was being taught how to jump. I felt quite confident that I could do it so I gave it a go. The approach went well, the Horse took off, and I didn't, and found myself hanging of the poor things neck, with the riding instructor screaming at me, sit up", sit up. When it became clearly obvious what was coming next, she changed that very quickly and shouted "abort, abort". So off the side of the Horse I fell straight onto my 'butt'.

We had battles and tears and tantrums, and he was forever taking the proverbial out of me, but I loved him so much that through hard work and determination things came good in the end and we achieved a good loving relationship.

We went to a fair few Show Jumping competitions, picking up various rosettes along the way. It was always the red ones you wanted as they would mean you had won your competition, with blue for second and yellow for 3rd. As we were new into competing, and couldn't jump at any reasonable height, we would regularly came up against young kids on very quick Ponies, and boy they were very fast and fearless. We did manage to get placed in various events but lining up to receive our prizes was very embarrassing as 'The Boy' was on the larger size, as was I, and we were forever looking downwards on the kids and their Ponies in the line up to receive our rosettes. Also I took a few tumbles and soon realised that falling off a Horse at an older age hurt a lot more than when you are younger.

So we moved into the world of Dressage, a discipline that required you to make precise movements at various points in an arena that were marked out with letters, and making sure you hit the markers with the right moves. I called upon the services of a different instructor, as it was a completely different discipline to jumping, and she helped us achieve outstanding results. We became very good very quickly, winning several rosettes, including the lovely red ones and winning local Championships, picking up several trophies and sashes. This was a surprise to us as he was not really a natural Dressage Horse, but boy he looked handsome when he was competing, and could carry himself immaculately, when he could be bothered!!! He was a black horse with little white socks on his back legs, and he gleamed in the arena. It would take two days to prepare for the competitions, cleaning the tack which the Horse had to wear, making sure my show clothes were up to scratch and bathing and grooming 'The Boy' but it was worth all the hard work in the end.

We had a good few years partaking in Dressage, but not wanting to compete in the same competitions every year and become what was known as a 'Trophy Hunter', we would need to move up to the next level of competition to carry on. Due to his age, and the fact he was starting to get Arthritis, we had to make the decision to retire him from competition, and just enjoy him for basic schooling and hacking. He was now reaching the grand old age of 20.

He had turned into the perfect gentleman and was pleasure to be around and everyone commented on how lovely and calm and perfect he was. If only they had seen him when he was younger!!!! He was a right little sod, but we loved him.

This is where the next part of the journey comes in!!

Chapter 2

Get Set...

MID LIFE CRISIS!!!!

As I have previously mentioned, I had always been very keen on athletics when I was at school. As the Horse was now retired, and even though I was still riding and really enjoying the leisurely schooling and walking out in the fields on him, I felt like I needed something else to get my teeth into. For years I had thought that I would love to have another go on the long jump just one more time, mainly to satisfy my curiosity. Now I was under no illusion that I would be any good, and was not interested in competitions, or to take it seriously, but I felt it was just something I wanted to get out of my system. I had been very good at the long jump at school, and just to at least have the chance to jump into the sandpit once again was very appealing, albeit maybe a little wacky.

We lived on the South East Coast of England, which was very renowned for beach holidays and day trips with people travelling from London and the Medway towns, but it was definitely not a hub for any sporting activities. The schools were pretty set up for most sports, but outside of that we were very limited. We had a few leisure complexes with swimming pools and gyms, but that was about it. Finding somewhere to satisfy my long-jump urge was going to be tricky.

However, by some twist of fate, we found a local club called Thanet Athletics Club. It was at the back of one of the local schools and to be honest with you we didn't even know it was there. It had been funded by the local Council so it was accessible through the club. My dream now seemed within reach, or so I thought. I had grandeur's of just turning up, having a chat and blasting my way down the runway and into the sand pit. Joy at last. We contacted them to see if they could help and to my shock and amazement, they said just to come along and have a chat with the Coaches and they would see what they could do for me.

So, in September 2017, at the grand old age of 56, I turned up at the local Athletics club, hoping for just a light session on the long jump to see how it went. The place was amazing. The track itself was of the same standard you see on the television, and had two long jump pits. It also had the cages for Throwing and a High Jump and Pole Vault area. It was everything you could have wanted and more.

The club was self-funding, and was run by a selection of Coaches who gave up their time freely, and would be there twice a week to train the Athletes, and they also give up their time in between to organise getting Athletes to competitions, making sure that everyone had the right paperwork to compete, and anything else that needed doing to ensure the smooth running of the club. They were all amazing and very welcoming. There was also a selection of volunteers who would also help the Coaches on training nights. It was a well-oiled machine, run by very dedicated people.

On arrival we met the sprints Coach called James, who had also previously been the Long Jump Coach, and I thought wow, what a bonus!! He soon scuppered my excitement when he said he was more than happy to help train me, but I couldn't go on the Long Jump until I got fitter. I thought I was quite fit until he asked me to jog 400 metres around the track. I looked around the track and thought, no problem. I almost collapsed after just 30 metres puffing and panting. That was very embarrassing. This was going to be a long hard slog and take a fair amount of time to achieve what I wanted to do, but I was determined and prepared to do whatever it took to fulfil my dream.

The club had a multitude of different age groups from very young to teenagers, and some seniors who were in their early twenties, but they didn't have a section for more mature aged athletes like me. I was going to be the one and only mature group!! I was to train with the teenagers and seniors, but I couldn't help thinking I would have been better off with the very young Athletes!!! I did get some very strange looks from the other Athletes, as they were all fit and healthy and very good at what they were trying to achieve. I was actually in awe watching them train, and you could see that they were very serious about what they were doing. They seemed to keep their distance but I don't know if that was because they were into the training session, or they just didn't know what to make of someone my age taking up Athletics. It must have seemed very strange.

The next few months were hard work and very painful. I must have pulled every muscle in my body, but a well-known brand of bath salts soon sorted that out, alongside anti-inflammatory's and muscle gels. I was training twice a week at the track, and also training at home as much as I could, purchasing a static bike, treadmill and any other accessories Coach James told me I needed, which included a kettle bell, a wobble board, which I kept falling off, and a variety of other items to enhance my training. I now fully understood the phrase "All the gear and no idea". Also, I found that the youngsters were warming to me, and offering advice and help where needed, although I still think they thought I was mad. I was becoming very fond of them, and was still in awe of what they were achieving. I did learn very quickly that there was no point trying to compete with them, as they were far too young and fit for that to happen. I had to find my own way and set my own goals and with Coaches' help, my training schedule was more tailored to my age and ability, but he still treated me the same as the other Athletes. Tim would also come to every session to be supportive, and he and James seemed to be striking up a friendship which was lovely to see. Tim had even started to help James with the training sessions, and even though he didn't seem at first to have a clue what he was doing, I secretly think he enjoyed it. I also think James was just glad to be able to talk to another adult!!!

Sprint training was going well but I had no illusions of competing in any way, shape or form, as it was just a means to an end to get on the long jump. It was lovely to hear and see the youngsters preparing for their competitions. They really did work hard and would get very excited before their big days arrived. We did pop along to some of the tracks they were competing at on several occasions to be supportive of them, and I must admit they all done really well picking up medals in their respective events. I was just so proud of them.

I was starting to get a lot fitter, and the day came when Coach finally let me loose on the Long Jump. You have to do a run up to work out how many strides you need to land on the board and launch yourself into the sand pit. So after warming up, we worked on my strides. When I was happy with them, Coach said "right, let's do this". So there I was, ready and primed to go, and very excited. I took off, counted my strides as I was running, launched myself, missed the board completely and landed flat on my butt!!! This was not going to be as easy as I thought. After a few more tries I started to get the hang of it, but it could have been better, and it became clearly obvious that a lot more Coaching was going to be needed on the Long Jump.

Although James was trying very hard to get me to compete, I didn't feel at my age that it would be possible, and I didn't want to make a fool of myself. So for a year I was more than happy just to turn up to training and support the youngsters when they were competing.

However, in September 2018, after being constantly bombarded by Coach to enter the club Championships, I thought, what the hell, why not just give it a go, and at least it would shut him up!!! I trained well and was actually getting quite excited about the thought of actually competing, albeit against myself. I must admit I was very nervous as I would be running and jumping against the youngsters, and I knew I had no chance of even getting close to them, but I had personal goals I wanted to achieve. The big day came and the track was buzzing with excitement. I prepared for my 100-metre race and Long Jump as best I could, and despite nerves kicking in I was actually looking forward to it. Lining up on the start line for the 100 metres was quite daunting to me as this was a whole new experience, but there I was, alongside my training partners ready to race against them. "Take your marks," feel sick, "Set" no idea what I'm doing, "Bang" and we were off!! OK, so I came last (expected) but I absolutely loved it!! The cheers and support I got from the crowd was amazing and made the whole experience worthwhile. Even the youngsters were cheering me on!

With my Adrenalin running very high it was off to the Long Jump. Again, it was amazing, and I had 4 good jumps, and actually managed to hit the board and landed respectfully in the pit, and I could not have been happier.

Who would have believed a year ago I would be in a competition? Not me for sure, but what an amazing day I had, and I cannot lie when I say I think I caught the competition bug.

The club Championships presentation night was held in December 2018, where the club hand out trophies and shields to the club champions and to the Athletes that have achieved outstanding performances throughout the year. I was shocked when I was awarded a small trophy for my achievements at the club Championships!! I must admit it bought a little tear to my eye, and I was so proud of myself. It was so lovely to see everyone else collect their trophies and watch them receive their shields for outstanding performances. Everyone worked so hard and they were all well deserved. I decided I wanted to get my hands on one of the shields next year!!

After receiving my trophy, it crossed my mind that I might just want to have a go at competing. The dilemma for me now was how I could possibly achieve this. There would be no point at all going up against the youngsters, but there really didn't seem to be anywhere to go with competitions for my age. Someone suggested having a look at what was called 'Master's Athletics'. What a game changer that would prove to be. It is designed for Athletes over 35 years of age, and competitions are in 5-year increments. So for me, I would be in the 55 to 59 age categories, and only competing against Athletes in that age group. At last I had found my calling. I joined a Masters club but was still a member of my local club. This was going to open up a whole new world of fun for me.

I carried on training even harder and done a lot of research into venues and competitions for the Masters and what was needed to take part. It was not going to be easy as there was nothing local so it would mean travelling a bit, but we were both happy to do this. There seemed to be quite a lot of competitions to participate in, and we planned meticulously what and where we wanted to go. To be honest with you, I wanted to do them all!! I really had got the bug.

Winter training has got to be the hardest thing ever. We were still training twice a week, and on several occasions we trained off track, sometimes running up hills, and on the beach, which was so hard to do, but apparently good for your fitness and stamina. I couldn't see it myself and found it painful and hard work. We had no indoor facilities, so all training was outside. The problem is you arrive wrapped up like a yeti, with multiple layers of clothes on, get hot, take them off, get cold and put them back on again. We trained in wind and rain but the worst had to be the snow!!! Not only was it cold, it was very wet as well. Coach James would not cancel any training sessions, and I have to admit we all turned up as usual, had a moan about the weather, and then just got on with it, and I have to admit you did feel a sense of achievement at the end of the sessions. But as the saying goes, no pain no gain. I liked to look at it as short-term pain for long term gain!!!

So, training done, research done, the indoor season mapped out, I was excited and confident that I could actually give this a go and start competing. Bring it on!!!!

LET THE GAMES BEGIN!!!!

My first Master's competition was held at Lee Valley Indoor Athletics stadium in North London on the 10th

February 2019 and was the Southern Counties Veteran Athletics Club Championships. It was an early start, and it would probably take us about two hours to drive there but we had given ourselves plenty of travel time so I was not worried about being late. We arrived very early and I was in awe of the venue. It was just so amazing and I could feel my confidence and excitement gaining momentum. Other Athletes started to arrive, and the atmosphere was buzzing. It was at this point I looked around me and my confidence took a huge battering. I could not believe how fit *ALL* of the other Athletes looked, all toned up and muscled, even those who were way above my age group, some of which were 80 years old and above!!! I thought I had trained hard enough and looked quite fit, but I could not have been more wrong!! Still, I was here now and was determined to at least give it a go.

The warm-up area was away from the main track and its very important to get the warm up right to maximise your potential to compete but as we wandered into it my jaw hit the floor. My God everyone was so fast and fit. I tried as hard as I could to go through my routine but couldn't take my eyes of the other Athletes. I just wanted to crawl into a corner and disappear. I had a set plan to complete my warm up but I was getting nowhere!! I tried my best but it wasn't happening.

I had entered the 60-metre sprint and the Long Jump. The 60-metres were up first, and I must admit I was absolutely 'bricking' it!!

My age group were called to the call room for the 60-metres, the area they hold you before you get to race, and I was put on a bench with 6 other Athletes that I would be racing against. My heart sank even further when I saw them. This was going to be embarrassing. We were led to the start line, I arranged my starting blocks to suit my getaway, and waited to be called to the line. "Take your marks", feel sick again "Set", still don't know what I am doing, "Bang!!!" And off they went with me following on way behind. One thing I learned on that day was that when it came to sprints, I was always going to be chasing 'butt'!! Needless to say, I was last, but there was a macabre side to me that actually enjoyed it and at least I had managed to survive my first race. Who would have believed it? This was going to be the first of many races and much 'butt' chasing. I had set what was called a personnel best time, but as this was my first ever 60-metre race that was inevitable. I would now at least have a time to improve on in the future.

My next event was the Long Jump. Again, I had no illusions of doing anything great, but was looking forward to it as this was really the main event I wanted to do. Again, the other Athletes were very fit in my age group, but everyone was very supportive and friendly when they realised this was my first competition. Learning how to do things properly was the hardest part, as there are certain protocols you must stick to, but that is where everyone was so helpful, and guided me through what I needed to do. I really was so very grateful for any help I could get!!

I measured out my run up with a tape measure, and put a marker down at the point I was going to start my run up. It was to be 14 strides and then jump off the board, making sure your foot doesn't go beyond the board as that would be a foul, but at this point I had no idea if that was going to be right or not. It was very different being indoors when all your training was outdoors. I had 2 practice jumps and managed to jump off the board and not put my foot over the fault line so I was happy enough. The competition began and I watched in awe at the other Athletes jumping. They were so good. Then it was my turn.

I stood by my marker, took a deep breath, and started my run up. To my surprise I hit the board perfectly, flew in the air and landed on the soft sand in the pit. It felt like a good jump, and to my absolute shock the jump had put me into 2nd place. This was now going to be a long competition. I watched with anticipation at everyone else's jumps, fingers crossed and living in hope, but no-one came close to what I had achieved. Not that I wished ill on anyone as they had all been so helpful, but I had a medal within my grasp and I so desperately wanted it!!! The competition finished and I had secured 2nd place picking up my first medal which was to be a Silver one. I must admit I had a little tear in my eye. I couldn't believe it, Tim couldn't believe it, and when I let Coach know he couldn't believe it either, but I think they were both very shocked and proud.

The drive home was great as I was still riding high on Adrenalin. We dissected everything, going through what went well, what didn't go well and what to do to move forward. Needless to say I slept well that night.

A week later we were back at Lee Valley for the South of England Masters Championships. Again, I had entered the 60 metres and the Long Jump. The 60 metres seemed to be following a pattern as again I was chasing 'butt' and came last but I did manage to clock another personnel best time. The long jump was next, and there were some familiar faces from the week before. As the age group is only 5 years, I learnt very quickly you could probably compete against the same Athletes a lot of the time.

I measured my strides, done my practice jumps and was happy. The competition began, and I was feeling good.

You get 6 jumps in all, so there's plenty of time to get it right, or wrong. I can't remember which jump it was, but one of the jumps itself was massive compared to what I had done previously. I knew it was good when I landed and I had achieved a huge personal best. I watched in anticipation again at everyone else's jumps and luckily for me no-one could match what I had done. I finished first and collected my first Gold medal with pride. I had now earned the title of South of England Masters Long Jump Champion!! Not bad for my second competition. Needless to say Tim, Coach James and I were all ecstatic!!

3 weeks later we were back at Lee valley again for the British Masters Championships, the biggest, best and main event of the indoor season. I thought the Athletes I had competed against already were amazing, but at the British Masters the Athletes come from all over the country and they are the cream of the crop. I could not believe how fit and fast they were. I must admit that on the day I was completely overawed by them and found it hard to concentrate let alone participate. I competed completely under par. I learned an invaluable lesson though. I have no control over what other Athletes do, but I am in control of my own destiny, and that is the only thing to concentrate on. This was to be a crucial learning curve that would take me forward in the future. The whole day was not wasted.

Chapter 3

Athletics.

2019, A GREAT YEAR!!!!!

2019 was to prove a very busy year for my Athletics. We had a lot of triumphs, tears and tantrums but never lost sight of the joy we were getting from competing.

My next major event was the Kent Championships on March 17th 2019, again held at the indoor stadium at Lee Valley. Now sadly this was not a Master's competition, but mainly designed for younger athletes, with events for all age groups, except mine, but again I buckled under pressure from Coach James and decided to give it a go. However, I was pleasantly surprised to see some of the friends I had made from the Masters meetings actually competing which made me feel a whole lot better and not so self-conscious.

The place was absolutely packed with very young excited Athletes, and the atmosphere was electric. Watching them do their warm ups was a real pleasure.

They had their Coaches with them, guiding them through their paces, and boy did they take it seriously.

Because of the vast range of ages with the youngsters, they separated Athletes into different age groups to compete, allowing for a level playing field. I watched, and cheered on a few of the Athletes from the club, and boy did they do well with some of them actually winning their respective events. Not bad for a small non-funded club competing with well-funded clubs from all over Kent. I was entered into the senior age group which I think was 21 and above (could be wrong but I can't quite remember).

The 60 metres went well, and yes, I was chasing 'butt'! But I almost ran personnel best which I was very pleased with. It was now onto the Long Jump. There were a lot of Athletes competing in this, but I didn't find out till later on that it was called a Tri Counties competition, where there was 2 other Counties competing for their own Championships as well as the Kent's being just the Kent competition. My jumps all went well, and I was really pleased with what I had done. I walked over to the officials at the end of the competition to thank them for all their hard work as this is the right thing to do, and I wanted to see the results which they had, and also congratulate all of the other jumpers on my way. To my absolute shock and amazement, I had won my competition (the Kent's). A lump came into my throat and I thought I was going to cry until it was pointed out to me that I was the only jumper in the Kent's competition!!

But as the saying goes, you've got to be in it to win it, and I would now hold the title of Kent Long Jump Champion for the next year. A fact that my Coach was very proud of!! This competition was the last of the indoor season, and I can honestly say that the whole experience of competing during the winter could not have gone any better. We would now be moving to outdoor competitions, a whole new ball game.

The first was to be the Kent's again, held at a beautiful outdoor venue called the Julie Rose Stadium in Ashford Kent. Again, as before, it was not a Master's competition. It was mainly for the youngsters, but by now I was just keen to compete, and it was great being outdoors.

The competition was held over 2 days, being the 11th-12th May and I got a bit carried away and entered 4 events, Long Jump, Discus, Javelin and 100 metres. I think I just got caught up in the moment. The Long Jump went well again and I managed to pick up 2nd place and a Silver medal, but again there was only 2 Athletes in my competition, and the winner was far younger and a much more superior jumper than me. We got on so well and really encouraged each other. She was having trouble with her run up, and it looked like she was going to do all no jumps which meant I would have won. I gave her some advice to help her; she listened, and managed a really good jump, winning the competition. I am competitive, but not at a price. I was actually really pleased for her. I didn't do very well in the other events, but had fun doing them, but lesson learned. Do not overdo it!!!

I was knackered by the end of the second day and felt like I would sleep for a week!!!

The club asked me to join them in a team competition in the Southern Athletics League. It was a series of five competitions held at several different locations in the South East with different teams from different clubs competing. I was a bit apprehensive as I knew I would have to compete against the young Athletes again, but it was pointed out to me that it was all about scoring points. As the club had been so good to me, I though why not give it a go.

They were to prove some of the best fun days out. As we were competing as a team, everyone was so supportive and encouraging, with us all travelling in a mini bus together. It was nice for me to get closer to the other Athletes, and I could sense some real bonding and friendships forming. It also gave me the chance to try out new discipline's as you could pretty much do which events you wanted to as it was all about point scoring. I did my standard sprints and jumps but also threw a Discus and a Javelin to help out. Didn't really care too much for the Javelin, but really enjoyed the Discus, so I decided to take that up as my 3rd competitive event. The only problem with the sprints was that instead of running 60 metres which I was used to, it went up to 100 metres. Those 40 metres extra seemed to take forever but I managed it, but boy was I whacked at the end of it!!! I competed in the Long Jump as normal, doing quite well and scoring good points for the team.

I did try the 200 metres at one of the meetings, achieving a personal best, but decided that this event was not for me at this moment in time.

During the rest of the year I helped at another 4 league meetings for the team. Although we scored some good points, we didn't do very well in the league, but we all had great fun attending them, and now I considered the young Athletes to be my friends, as I think they did of me.

We resumed our Masters competitions again in May and we travelled to the beautiful City of Oxford for the Southern Counties Veteran Athletics Championships at a venue called Tilsey Park. We decided on this occasion to actually arrive the night before and stay over in a hotel, as the competition was to start early and we wanted to arrive refreshed and awake.

I had decided again to enter the Long Jump, 100 metres and have a go at the Discus, this being my first Master's competition in this event. In Master's competitions, there are certain standards you have to meet to receive a medal, and I had worked hard to try and reach the required distance for the Discus but was not overly confident. I could do it at home but competing is a whole new kettle of fish!!! Also, this was going to be my first Master's 100 metre race.

First event was the Long Jump, which by now I was starting to feel quite confident with (but not cocky). There were some good jumpers, and the competition was strong, but again I managed to jump into first place, picking up another Gold medal!!! The 100 metres was next. They had decided to run the race with different age groups due to lack of competitors, so now I would be running against younger and older Master's athletes whilst still only competing in my age group!! It can be very confusing. So, we were called to the start line. I looked around me and though going to be chasing 'butt' again!!! "Take your marks," at this point I tried to breath and focus on the task at hand, looking down the track and beyond the finish line focusing on how I wanted my run to go. I couldn't help thinking though it looked a long way compared to the 60 metres I was used to doing indoors. "Set," big deep breath, and lower into the blocks, making sure you feel comfortable in them. "Bang" and we are off!!! Yup, you've guest it, I was chasing 'butt' again, but I wasn't last and managed to actually beat another Athlete in my age group and pick up another Gold medal!!!

We moved onto the Discus, and I must admit I was very nervous. I knew I had to throw 16 metres or above to have any chance of doing well. I had achieved this at home training on several occasions, but now didn't feel that confident. Standing in the throwing circle with Discus in hand, I felt like everything was closing in on me, and all my mental thoughts went completely out of the window. You get 4 throws and my first 2 throws were absolutely abysmal. I took a bit of a verbal battering from Tim who was trying to get me motivated. It helped, and my 3rd throw was better but still short of the 16 metres

I needed. In my head I had blown it. One more throw. I walked into the circle, looked out onto the throwing field, visualised where I wanted the Discus to go, and relaxed and done some deep breathing. I then wound myself up to throw the Discus and released it. It seemed like an eternity before the Officials measured it and shouted back the result to the Official "16 metres 01". I nearly fainted!! I had done it, albeit by the skin of my teeth, and felt so proud and relieved when they announced I had finished second picking up a Silver medal. Talk about cutting it fine. A lot of valuable lessons were learnt that day, not to put too much pressure on oneself and relax. As I said before, you can only be in control of what you do and not what everyone else does. Think Tim was quite proud as well.

Another great day out and the drive home de-brief was great. We discussed what went well, what didn't go so well, and things to improve on next time. These de-briefs were to become a very vital part in all competitions, so I would know what to do next time or not do, to build on what could be improved, which for me was almost everything!!!

We were off to Kingston upon Thames next in July, for the Veteran Athletics Club Championships. A beautiful Stadium but boy it was a hot day!! Again, I had entered the 3 events with which now I was comfortable. First up came the 100 metres. Things were done a little different as they ran the races in seeding's, going by your personal best times, which meant I was running against older Athletes, not the ones in my age group. Bit weird, but boded well as I won my race posting a personal best time!!!! It was actually nice to cross the line first!! No chasing 'butt' this time!! Another very vital lesson was learnt this day. As an older Athlete, certain functions in the body are not as strong as they used to be. I had discovered in races before that the Bladder could leak a little but had not paid too much attention to it. Hindsight is a wonderful thing, and on this particular day I wish I had given my Bladder the respect it was starting to demand!

To my horror my Bladder let go slightly, and a trivial follow through from the Bowel decided to adorn me as I crossed the finish line. I was mortified to say the least. As luck had it, I carried spare knickers and baby wipes in my kit bag. If I hadn't, it would have been a short day out and a long drive home.

I also learned it was a good idea to always wear lady pads for leakage when competing or training. Lesson learned. Oh, and by the way, I managed to finish 2nd in my actual age group for the 100 metres and another Silver medal!!

I did manage to pick up another Gold medal in the Long Jump, but again I was the only competitor (got to be in it to win it) and then we were off to the Discus again. I was looking forward to this as I felt happier than before and was keen to try out a new throwing technique which we had worked on at home. So, into the throwing cage I went, feeling a lot more confident than last time. The first 2 throws were again abysmal, and obviously thoughts turned to my last competition with the Discus and feeling like here we go again. Throw number 3 was next.

I walked into the cage, stood at the back and took several deep breaths to calm myself down. I looked out over the field and visualised where I wanted my Disc to go. A few more deep breaths and I felt at ease. Into the circle I went, steadied myself to throw, staying calm, spun round and let the Disc go with all my might. BOOM!!! It flew!! I knew straight away it was a good throw and was jumping up and down with excitement, much to the amusement of the other Athletes. Throw measured, I waited in anticipation for my distance. 18 metres 17 bellowed from the Official. I had managed a massive personnel best and a huge improvement on last time. To say I was over the moon was an understatement, and Tim was so proud. He had worked hard to help me both physically and mentally with the Discus and it had paid off. I couldn't thank him enough. I won the competition picking up Gold. It had been another long day but a good one. Again, the drive home was fruitful, de-briefing everything. A lot of positives came out from today.

THE BIG ONE.

The biggest outdoor Master's competition of the year was the British Master's Championships, and this year it was held at the Alexander Stadium in Birmingham in August, a venue that had seen several Elite Athletes compete over the years.

It was held over two days, so consequently it meant a two night stay in a Hotel. I wasn't sure I wanted to go, as I still thought I could not do myself justice against the top Master's athletes in the country but buckled under pressure again from Coach James and Tim and decided to give it a go. I had entered the Long Jump and 100 metres which were on the Saturday and the Discus was on the Sunday. We arrived at the stadium on the Saturday and I was overawed again by what I saw. The fitness of some Master's Athletes can be Mind blowing when you see them. Also, being at a venue which had been adorned by Elite Athlete's messed with my head a little. I was walking (running jumping and throwing) in the footsteps of some of the country's finest Elite Athletes.

The 100 metres and the Long Jump were both scheduled at exactly the same time. Again, this messed with my head as I could not work out how the hell I was going to manage that. This was a new experience to me and I was getting stressed about it. One of the other female Athletes who were also doing both events seemed to notice my anxiety. She was a very experienced competitor and had obviously encountered this problem before. She was amazing with me, explaining the best way to deal with the situation. She advised to go to the Long Jump first, work out the run up, change to running spikes, run the 100 metres, go back to Long Jump, and change to jumping shoes and then jump!! Sounds easy enough, but with nerves and Adrenalin pumping, trust me it wasn't.

I managed to mark out my run up on the Long Jump, and done a practice jump, but I wasn't happy with it, and I needed to get to the 100-metre start line ASAP. So here we go again. "Take your marks." Deep breath, look down the track to the finish line, visualise going beyond the line. "Set." Lower into the starting blocks, getting comfortable. Then lower head ready to run. "Bang" And we were off!!! And yes, you've guessed it, chasing 'butt' again, but I did manage to post a personal best which given the situation was quite amazing.

No time for rest, it was a quick return back to the Long Jump. Now in the Masters you get 6 jumps. As long as you have a valid jump in the first 3, you get the chance to complete the last 3 jumps. I had been worried about my run up and with good reason. I fouled my first 2 jumps!!! Only one more left and if I didn't get a jump in, my competition would be over. I prepared myself, looked down the runway, and ran. I could tell I was going to foul, so slowed down my run and stuttered to try and get on the board. I managed to hit the board, and literally haul myself into the sand pit. I looked back at the board judge and was relieved to see the white flag. A red one would have been a disaster. I had a legal jump. However, it was the worst jump in distance I had jumped since I started the Long Jump again, but at least I had 3 more jumps. As expected, I didn't finish in the medals, but a lot of lessons were learned today which would bode well in the future, and thanks to the kindness and caring of the other Athlete who helped me, I had sort of coped with the situation. I could not thank her enough.

Sunday bought us back to the Stadium for the Discus. I realised that the competition was fierce as I knew pretty much what the other Athletes could throw, and I was nowhere near them in distance. But I took this time just to gain experience, relax and enjoy myself. Again, being the Masters, you get 6 throws. All my throws seemed to go well and I had already surpassed my personnel best with a 20-metre throw!!

On my next throw, I prepared myself as usual, spun round to release the Disc and let out an almighty roar as I did so. The Disc seemed to fly forever!!! Imagine my shock when the distance came back at 22 metres 66!! The loveliest thing was that all the other Athletes applauded me, and one of the Officials actually apologised and stated that he thought I was going to be rubbish but admitted he was wrong. Cheeky bugger!!

I came 4th in the competition, narrowly missing out on a medal, but Tim and I could not have been prouder of what I had achieved. Again, the drive home was fruitful, albeit a long drive, but we both agreed we had enjoyed the most wonderful weekend, and a lot of lessons were learned.

On a beautiful sunny and warm September morning our next meeting was the Kent Masters Championships held in Erith Kent over two days. The venue was only an hour away from home so it didn't really demand an early start, but we did leave early anyway as you never know about traffic and I like to arrive early at a venue to get to know the surrounding's and be a part of the atmosphere building. This time around I decided it was time to give the 200 metres another go. I hadn't trained hard for this, but felt with my fitness improving over the summer; it would be a chance to see how I would fair with it. So on the Saturday I was to run the 200 metres and throw the Discus, and then return on the Sunday to run in the 100 metres. The Long Jump was to be held the following week at a different venue.

The Kent masters is the only competition that links the ages in ten-year gaps, so on this occasion I would be competing against athletes from fifty to fifty-nine instead of fifty-five to fifty-nine. Why it was done this way, nobody knew, but I had entered knowing this so decided just to take my chances.

The Discus was my first event on this day, and I knew the competition was going to be hard. I had studied the form of the other throwers and felt that if I got it right on the day I could be in with a chance of a medal, but nothing is a given. We had six throws each and everybody threw very well. I only managed 2 legal throws, much to the disgust of Tim and Coach but I managed a throw of 20 metres 98 finishing second and receiving a Silver medal.

Next up on the Saturday was the 200 metres. This was going to be hard as I had not run one for a while and the weather seemed to be getting hotter. I was starting to doubt my sanity. As there were only a few Athletes over various age groups entered they decided to run everyone together covering all eight lanes. I think in my age group there were three of us. As I stood on the start line, I looked around the track and was shocked when I realised how far it was. This was not going to be easy.

"Take your marks." Here we go again, now with butterflies. I tried not to think too hard about the distance but when I looked again my stomach churned. "Set," down in the blocks and just try and hold it together. "BANG" I started well and ran a good bend. About 50 metres from the line the wheels came of, and I hit what they call 'the wall'. This is where you have run out of everything and just running on pure adrenaline. Not a good feeling because as hard as you try, there's just nothing left in the tank to run with. I made it to the line, crossed the line and sank to my knees. It took a couple of minutes to get my breath back, but I had done it and although exhausted felt quite proud of myself. I had come 2nd in my age group, and achieved another Silver medal.

On the drive home we analysed the 200 metres, and I decided that through winter training I would work on it as I felt this would be a good discipline for me to do. We also dissected my Discus and I got a lot of huffs and puffs from Tim, admittedly deserved.

We arrived back in Erith on the Sunday for what was to be my only event that day, the 100 metres. I was feeling a little tired from the Saturday. But it was only

100 metres!! Stupid way of thinking, there's no only about it. There were only three of us in my race, the other 2 Athletes being of the fifty to fifty-five age group putting me at a bit of a disadvantage. We lined up. God I was tired. "Take your marks." Just need to stay awake and run. You can do it.

"Set" Seemed to take forever to get into the blocks, "BANG." And here we go again!!! There is such a thing as overdoing it, and I think this weekend had taken its toll on me. However, I ran a decent race, chased 'butt' all the way and as expected finished third. To say I was relieved it was over was an understatement. I had pushed myself to my limits this weekend. The drive home was a lot quieter than normal. I was just too exhausted to speak.

The following weekend saw the Kent Masters Long Jump Championships held in Medway. Why this was separated from the main championships last weekend no-one knows, but the nice thing was that it was at the same venue as the Kent (younger Athletes) Relay Championships which a couple of teams from our club had entered. The atmosphere at the venue was electric with a lot of very excited young relay teams. Boy they were good!!! And fast.

So onto the Long Jump, again, they let all the Athletes from all age groups compete at the same time which was nice as there were about 10 of us, and we would have decent breaks in between jumps. There were only 3 in my age group, again the other 2 being in the fifty to fifty five age groups. I managed a good jump but needless to say, I came third, but as a competition I really enjoyed it. All of us Athletes got on so well and encouraged each other to the end, and I felt that some friendships had been forged and looked forward to seeing some of them again in the future. Was great watching the relays as well? Took me back to my school days!!!

There wasn't much to talk about on the way home and actually for once it was nice not to dissect what had gone on. There really wasn't that much to dissect. I think we were both happy just to revel in what a great day we had.

Just to get every last ounce of energy out of myself, I decided to enter the Club Championships the week after, and God only knows why, but I entered 4 events, being 100 metres, Long Jump, Discus and Javelin. I would be the only Master's Athlete in all competitions, but this was the final meeting of the season and wanted to go out with a bang!!!! Again, the atmosphere was electric as there were all age groups competing from extremely young to myself, starting to feel very old!! I managed to do well in all my events, posting a personal best in the 100 metres which according to Coach was ridiculous being so late in the season and the fact I was running into a very strong wind. I also managed a personal best in the Javelin. I won all my events, but it wasn't about that. I had experienced the most amazing season and didn't want it to end. I was proud of myself for just getting out there and having a go, and amazed at just far I had come, and how well I had done. I thought I was just going to make a fool of myself at the beginning of the season, but this could not have been further from the truth. It goes to prove a point; if you are determined you can achieve almost anything. Tim and Coach James were very proud of me as well.

PRESENTATION NIGHT.

Thanet Athletics Club held their annual presentation night in December 2019. With a party style atmosphere, everyone was excited in anticipation of where the Trophies and Shields were going to go this year. Tables were laid with decorations and nibbles, and there was to be a Buffet later in the evening. A big screen was also showing snippets of what Athletes had done during the season. Some were outstanding to watch, others a little more comical.

The evening started with a speech from the then Chairman, praising everyone for working so hard to make the presentation night happen, and re-iterated at how well the club had done over the last year. The club is small, and all of the Coaches and support team are volunteers and give up their time freely. Without them there would be no club. There then came a speech from the head Coach Darren, who again gave homage to everyone for the last year, and he spoke about some of the amazing achievements by most of the Athletes, and outlined plans moving forward for 2020. It was going to be a great year!!!

The time came to present the Trophies for the club Championship day, held back in the summer to the Athletes, and the excitement built. As the age range was from 6-7-years up to seniors this was going to take some time, but to see the faces on all the Athletes as they collected their trophies was well worth it. Smiling seemed to be the order of the day. It came to the senior section (after what seemed to be an eternity) and you can only imagine my delight when my name was read out to receive the Trophies for Sprints, Long Jump and Discus!!! I was over the moon and accepted my Trophies with huge delight and to rapturous cheers and applause from everyone in the room. The buffet came next, which again was made by the Coaches and helpers at the club and it was an absolute feast, and very welcome as I think we were all getting a bit peckish by this point.

What was considered to be the highlight of the evening came next, the presentation of the Shields. These are judged by all of the Coaches and given to the Athletes who had achieved outstanding performances throughout the year, going over and above their capabilities and exceeding expectations. Again, the presentations started with the younger Athletes first, and to see the faces of the winners was an absolute joy. We moved onto the senior section. I sat with my fingers crossed and my eyes closed. My heart was racing and my palms sweaty. It felt like the start of a race!!! "And this year's shield for senior Sprints goes to" It was me!!!!!!! I had done it!! What seemed like impossibility this time last year had actually come true. I walked up to the Chairman to receive my Shied and promptly burst into tears. I walked back to the table with such pride I thought I was going to burst. "And this year's Shield for Senior Jumps goes to" it was me again!!! No sooner had I sat down I was up again, receiving my second Shield. So, I walked back up to the Chairman again to receive my shield and promptly burst into tears again. I had not only done what I could only have dreamt of a year earlier, I had done it twice! If happiness could have been bottled and sold, I would have been a Millionaire on this amazing night. The evening had been a complete success for everyone involved and especially for me. What had started as a little go on the Long Jump had turned into a passion and desire to be better, faster and stronger. It had been a tough journey with a steep learning curve, with tears, tantrums and tribulations, not to mention a plethora of injuries, but it was all worth it in the end. We were all now to take a well-earned Christmas break and resume training in 2020. Wow!! That was some year.

In Athletics there is a web site called the Power of Ten. It is basically designed so you can see how well you are doing in the country in your age category and the ultimate accolade is to be in the top ten in your chosen events. It is also useful when competing against other Athletes as you can see what their standard is, which gives you an idea as to how you would fair against them in competition. Needless to say, in the 50-59 female categories, the cream of the crop occupied the top spots. Looking at their times and distances, I would have struggled to beat them even when I was at school!!

However, it is with pride that I would like to share my achievements with you.

Indoors I managed to finish 16th out of 18 in the 60 metres, 14th out of 14 in the 200 metres and 7th out of 11 in the Long Jump.

Outdoors I managed to finish 28th out of 78 in the 100 metres, 37th out of 81 in the 200 metres, 9th out of 81 in the Discus and 9th out of 65 in the Long Jump. Two top 10 places. BOOM!!!!!

I think and hope you will agree, not a bad first season. Bring on 2020!!!!!!!!!!!!!!!!!!!!!!!!!!!!!!!!!!

Chapter 4

Covid 19.

2020, A GREAT START!!!!

"HAPPY NEW YEAR" and welcome to 2020!!! We had the most amazing Christmas and spent the festive holidays with my Dad and Audrey in Ipswich. They had spent last year with us, so it was decided we would go to them this year. They could not have made us feel more welcome!! We followed with family tradition, and at 11am on Christmas day we opened the first of many bottles of Sherry and plated the mince pies. The tradition being we raise a glass and eat a mince pie to dearly departed family and friends, with other family members joining us on the phone. It's not a sombre thing, but a celebration of their lives. Remember our loved ones in a very fitting way. We ate loads, drank loads and played loads of games. Christmas dinner was delicious preceded by probably a little too much Sherry, especially on my Dad's part, but it didn't spoil the enjoyment of the feast. Sleeps were the order of the day following dinner. They had also arranged a beautiful buffet on Boxing Day with all of Audrey's family attending which was so much fun, and lovely to see them all. Then it was time to leave. It all goes far too quickly, but we were still both excited as we were having another Christmas Day with all our personal presents when we got home.

Our Christmas day at home was just as magical. You wouldn't have realised it wasn't Christmas Day as we done everything as if it was the real deal. We opened our presents, and Tim prepared a sumptuous dinner. My job before Christmas is to buy in everything we need, making sure nothing is missed. I must admit I do go over the top a little, but it's a precise art done with military precision and I truly love doing it. Tim then takes over on Christmas day and creates a masterpiece in culinary delights, a feat that he adores, and I must admit is outstandingly good at.

More food, more drinks, more games and more sleeps. Our Christmas dinner at home can last up to 3 hours. We do like to get our money's worth. We normally start eating around 2ish with the starter, followed by the main event. We then play a few games at the table and by this time it is usually dark. That's when the lighting of the pudding happens. A major highlight for any Christmas dinner and very tasty when soaked in brandy. We spent time re-living the year that had gone and agreeing how amazing it had been. We had bought each other very different presents for Christmas this year, from special days out, tickets to the London Athletics games and also for several concerts that we both wanted to see. We talked about holidays especially camping which is something we both love and holidays with hot tubs nestled in the heart of the forests.

New Year's Eve was another great night, starting with canapés and drinks, followed by a sumptuous meal that lasted for hours. We played games, drank more and saw in the New Year with Champagne and party poppers! We again talked about the year ahead and how grateful we were for all the things we had to look forward to. We said how much fun it was going to be. Who could have guessed at this point how wrong we were going to prove to be.

WINTER TRAINING, BRUTAL!!!

Festivities over, it was time to return to the track for winter training. Cold, wet damp evenings play hell with the joints when your, let's just say, a little older than all of the other Athletes, but with a good warm up session, the muscles soon get to work. It's just getting started that's the hard part.

I had decided to concentrate on the 200 metres this season, as I felt this would be an event I could possibly do quite well at. Coach didn't seem too keen at first but we decided to give it a go. It was hard going, but I was making progress which was the main thing. Sadly, several sessions had to be cancelled due to ice and snow, which was very unusual as James hated to have to cancel anything, but I felt I was still getting in some constructive training and was very keen to carry on. I also managed to pull several muscles, and pulled my hip joint, but luckily they were not to serious and my recovery was swift.

So, we were off to our first indoor competition of the year at the beginning of February. It was the Southern Counties Veteran Athletics Club Championships held at Lee Valley Stadium in North London. I had decided not to enter the 200 metres at this meeting, as I felt I was not quite ready. I would save myself for the next competition. At this point I had noticed a very slight fluttering in my heart. It wasn't bad and only very slight so I didn't really pay too much heed to it and put it down to probably over training. More rest was going to be needed I think, but I was just so keen to do well, that I dismissed the problem. My bad! I had entered the 60 metres, and once again you've guessed it, I was still chasing 'butt' but managed to finish second in the Long Jump. A good start to the year we both agreed on the way home.

A week later we were off again to Lee Valley for the South of England Master's Championships, where I had decided to enter the 60 metres, Long Jump and finally have a go at the 200 metres. The fluttering in my heart was still there on and off, but again I wasn't too concerned as it didn't seem to be impeding me in training or competing.

The morning went well, and I felt good. The 60 metres was like Deja- vu ('butt' chasing again), but I managed again to achieve a second place in the Long Jump. The 200 metres was not scheduled until the afternoon, so I had plenty of time to relax, eat food and re-hydrate.

The time had come to warm up for the 200 metre competition, and I must admit I was feeling very nervous about the race. I had really trained hard for this one and didn't want anything to go wrong. During warm up, I felt a little tired, and my breathing wasn't as good as I was happy with, but I put it down to my anxiety. We were called to the 'call room' where they hold you before your event. There were quite a few races, so the wait seemed to go on forever, and my nerves were rising to the point I wasn't so sure I could do it. Looking back in hindsight it was at this point I really should have pulled out, but I was just so keen to try the 200 metres that all logic went out of the window. Hindsight is a wonderful thing isn't it?

The time came, and my race was called to the start line. Again, I didn't seem to feel right, and I noticed that I was a little 'out of sorts' but again I thought that nerves and anxiety were to blame. We were called to the blocks, and the starter took his position. "Take your marks", something really didn't feel right. "Set" settling into the blocks, but something is still wrong, but got to focus, and "Bang", we were off.

The first half of the race went well, but then to my shock and horror I lost all of my energy and was flagging badly. I couldn't pick myself up, and despite the cheering and encouragement from the other watching Athletes, I felt weaker and weaker.

Something was very wrong, and I was being left behind by Athletes a lot older than myself. I managed to cross the line in less than a respectable time and felt very ill.

I managed to crawl off the track and found a safe place to lie down as I had gone very weak to the point I almost fainted. I don't think anyone saw me, so I raised my legs and done some very deep breathing. The faint feeling passed, and I managed to get back to the call room and collect my things. The journey home was interesting as we always talk about what went well, what didn't go so well, and what could be done better next time. We put the problem with the 200 metres down to over training for it and getting far too anxious about the race. Needless to say, we both could not have been more wrong.........................

In January, there were mutterings of a bug that was circulating in a place called Wuhan and the Government suspended all travel to China. They called it Coronavirus. The first cases were confirmed in the UK at the end of January 2020.

In February it was becoming very serious over there, to the point Wuhan had gone into lock-down, and we were told to be a little more vigilant in this country, being advised to look out for symptoms, being a persistent or new cough and a fever, and taking care with hand washing and avoiding physical contact with people. This is where the handshake was made redundant and the elbow and fist pump were the order of the day. No one at this point seemed overly concerned.

COVID 19.

At the beginning of March we were again back at Lee Valley in North London for the British Masters Championships. This was to be a two-day event, so we decided to stay overnight. My heart fluttering was still there but it hadn't got any worse so just decided to see how it went. The Saturday saw me compete in the 60 metres (chasing 'butt' again) and the Long Jump. No medals this time but I was really pleased with my efforts, seeing as again I was competing against the cream of the crop.

I had pre-entered the 200 metres and the Discus for the Sunday, and given the disaster I had experienced on my last 200 metres, we both decided that at this point I would withdraw from the race. This could have be seen as giving in or giving up, but I saw it more as protecting myself from harm and would return to the 200 metres when I went back to training.

Although these Championships were an indoor event, obviously the Discus was held outside. Needless to say, the weather could not have been worse!! We only had 4 throws each, and I swear that every time I entered the throwing circle it rained on me harder than it did on everyone else!! I don't think this was the case, but it felt like it. I didn't throw well at all. I kept slipping and the Discus just didn't seem to want to play today. I managed a meagre throw of 19 metres 11 which was very disappointing as I was now becoming a regular 21 metre plus thrower. I was lying in third place, but then the last thrower threw just over 20 metres, relegating me to 4th place. To say I was gutted was not an exaggeration.

I had thought I was in with a chance of my fist British Masters medal but was robbed at the last moment. Back to the drawing board!

The Coronavirus situation was now getting more sombre, with people in our country contracting it and becoming very ill. At this point sadly a few people had lost their lives to the disease, which had now been given its correct scientific name of Covid 19. With infection rates rising every day there was talk that the NHS would struggle to cope should it take hold over here as it had in China. Testing had started for Covid 19 and it was confirmed that people travelling to the UK form abroad had contracted it. It was getting a lot more serious.

We were due to go to the Kent Championships on the 15th March, but there was talk on the grapevine it may have to be cancelled. It was decided by the powers to be to let the event go ahead and advised everyone on social distancing and hand washing. This was going to be some task as the event was again mainly aimed at the younger Athletes and the fear was they would not comprehend what was going on. And I really don't think they did, as many of us didn't at the time. The venue was packed, with a buzz of excitement ringing around the building. I had again entered the 60 metres and Long Jump, but again being a Master's Athlete against youngsters, my expectations were not high. There were only two of us in the Long Jump, so I finished second, but I did manage a season's best jump. This was really pleasing as it was going to bode well for the rest of the season. The 60 metres was to prove very interesting. There were two heats and I was in the second heat.

I ran a good race, and to my shock, horror and bewilderment I made the final!! I would have to run again, and I was knackered!! My Coach thought it was hilarious, but I didn't share his enthusiasm at this point. So, "Take your marks" I can do this, I looked down the track beyond the finish line, "Set" lowered myself into the blocks and took a deep breath, 'BANG,' and off they went, and yes by now you get the picture, I was chasing 'butt.' However, my time was respectable, and I was very proud of myself as were Tim and Coach James. Not much to de-brief on the way home, as to be honest I was too knackered to have any brain stuff thrown at me, but we agreed it had been a good day.

This was the last indoor event for the 2020 season, and in fact, sadly it was to prove to be the last meeting of the whole year.

SOMETHINGS WRONG!!!

I had continued to train whilst competing during the winter, but was noticing that the fluttering in my heart was now turning into more like palpitations, and I was getting short of breath and going slightly lightheaded. It was very intermittent, but I was more than aware of it. I didn't mention it to Tim at this point as I didn't want to worry him and thought maybe I was just over doing it again. The other worry was that the Coronavirus was now taking hold all over the country and becoming very serious. It was said that it was a disease that affected the chest and caused breathing problems. The stories being brandished about were starting to sound horrific, as more cases were being confirmed every day and sadly more people were losing their lives. This started to considerably worry me and caused me to have a few sleepless nights thinking I was going to catch, or already had it, and this was the cause of my breathlessness and being light headed. Again, I could not have been more wrong.

8 days after the last competition, a national UK lockdown was announced on 23rd March 2020. This bought an abrupt end to everything. No training, no travel, no days out, the hospitality industry was shut down, as well as gyms and hair and beauty salons and anything else that was classed as non-essential. People were told they must stay at home, and only to leave for essential items like shopping, medicines, and to travel to and from work if working from home was not an option. The police were given powers to enforce these new rules.

People started to panic buy items from the supermarkets, with toilet rolls being the main problem followed by eggs, flour and pasta and a variety of other products. Apparently banana bread was the big bake of the day!!! You could see on the News, trolley loads of the said items being wheeled out of the stores, which meant that a lot of people were missing out!! The situation was ridiculous, but after a short while the supermarkets put a cap on how many of the goods you could buy in one go. Great move by them and a lot fairer on everyone else.

The Government introduced what they called the Furlough Scheme whereby they would pay 80% of employees' wages up to £2,500 to try and help protect people's jobs and a host of other measures to help businesses. I was still working, but I was given 3 weeks off on Furlough, which at that time I was grateful for as I didn't particularly feel safe at work. In fact, I felt unsafe everywhere.

It was said that the NHS was becoming overwhelmed with the situation, and finding it hard to cope with the demand on them due to Covid 19. On the 26th March the first 'Clap for Carers' took place and was to continue for several weeks. We were all asked to stand outside our houses at 8pm every Thursday and Clap or make as much noise as possible. Some people Clapped, others were banging pots and pans, and a gentleman over the back of our house even put on some loud music to mark the occasion. I must admit the whole situation with the Clapping caught me out a little as I got a little emotional at the magnitude of the situation and felt a little silly. However, when we returned indoors it seemed I was not the only one. I think the response to the 'Clap for Carers' touched a lot of people.

I was now starting to get a heavy thumping in my chest which was starting to get unpleasant and was lasting for about 2 hours at a time and then would stop. The breathlessness and light-headed feeling were still there but didn't seem any worse. It was just the thumping in my chest that was the most problematic. It wasn't stopping me from doing anything as I continued to train at home and at the park, as that was allowed on my own with Tim under the lock-down rules, with Coach James setting the sessions for me, but I was getting more concerned, so at the beginning of April I decided to tell Tim about it. I don't think he was too happy I hadn't told him sooner, but I really didn't want to worry him. Stupid of me really as we work so well as a team, and never have any secrets! I did feel extremely guilty about that one and vowed never to hold anything from him again. We decided to phone the Doctors to explain the situation. A lot of people were very sceptical about contacting their Doctors because of the Pandemic and were worried about putting added pressure on them, but we decided that something needed to be done. We didn't really expect anything to happen because of Covid 19, but the Doctor recommended I attend the surgery the same day for an

ECG. The ECG showed what was called slight AF (Atrial Fibrillation) and the Doctor was going to arrange for a 24-hour heart monitor to be fitted, but said it could take weeks before it happened because of the Pandemic.

A few days later on the 18th April I had the worst thumping yet which resulted in me fainting due to being light headed and my breathing was not too good. We phoned 111 for advice and they recommended a trip to A&E, which again I was concerned about because of Covid 19.

I had to go alone as they were not allowing people to accompany patients because of the Virus. They confirmed AF and they were very concerned about my heart rate as it was extremely fast. They were just about to give me some drugs to bring it back to a normal level when it stopped abruptly (the thumping, not my heart)!! And I felt back to normal. It had lasted two hours.

The Doctor joked that I was a self-healing patient. I wish! A chest X ray was done and bloods taken but they came back all clear, so I was discharged and marched myself off home with a skip in my step feeling great. A report was to be sent to the Doctors and I was to call them to let them know what had happened, which I did, and they said thank you for letting them know. No follow up was arranged!!

A few days later I had another thumping episode which again lasted 2 hours and kept me awake at night which did annoy me as I do like my sleep!! This prompted another call to the Doctors where it was agreed I should start on what they called Beta Blockers which are designed to slow the heart rate down. At this point it was just a telephone consultation as they were not allowing patients to actually attend the Surgery. I was to have another blood test before starting the medication. It came back normal, but it was mentioned that something was slightly raised but it was nothing to worry about and no further action was required. I also mentioned that I had a slight pain in the right hand side of my chest but was told it was probably not related to my problem. If only I had questioned these things more. The worrying thing was, they were still waiting for the ECG from the A&E department at the Hospital so they could determine what they were dealing with. They also agreed to refer me to a Cardiologist.

I must admit I was starting to regret training so hard for the 200 metres, but that was to prove the least of my problems, as it became obvious and clear further down the line that it was not that which had caused the situation.

A week later I took a call from the Doctors stating that I was to start on Anti-Coagulants, a blood thinning medication, to prevent me from having a stroke!! Talk about panic setting in!!! I imagined all sorts of things going wrong!!! The brain is a very fickle thing when told something like that and my thoughts were not very kind to me!!!

The 24-hour monitor was fitted, and the results came back as stable. Some good news at last!!!

A few days later I noticed my face and neck had started to swell slightly and my breathing was getting a little worse. I had another telephone consult with the Doctors and they changed my Beta Blockers as they thought I was having an allergic reaction to the ones I was on. A few days went by and the swelling got worse to the point I thought my head was going to explode!! Another telephone consult and the Beta Blockers were changed again!!! The swelling was getting progressively worse so again I called the Doctors, had another telephone consult, and was given Anti Histamines which after a few days made no difference, so once more the Beta Blockers were changed. I really didn't think the medication was working but not being medically trained I took the advice I was given. At this point I had not been physically seen by anyone. Again, this was down to Covid 19 as all Consults were conducted by telephone.

I tried to continue training at home, but this was becoming harder and harder due to the breathing problem and the face swelling, but no-one had told me not to train so I just carried on. Running was becoming almost impossible as I was getting out of breath really quickly. We had managed to find somewhere to throw the Discus but again this was proving difficult as every time I bent down to pick the Disc up my face would swell!! But I soldiered on like a complete idiot!!!

The appointment came through with the Cardiologist for the 22nd June, and again it was a telephone Consult. It would have been nice to actually see him, but I fully understood the predicament we were in with Covid 19. He did seem nice, and we had a long conversation, with him mainly asking a lot of questions, and plenty of emphasis being put on the face and neck swelling and the breathing problem. He arranged for me to have an emergency scan, and to my surprise it was done 4 days later. Getting the results were going to prove problematic, as I was advised to call the Cardiologists Secretary to obtain them. I phoned and was told to get back in touch with the Doctors who would have to send an Electronic Advisory Notification (whatever that was) to the Consultant. The secretary also told me that the Consultant had not viewed the results and would not be able to for at least another week.

This caused us both much distress as we were now in a situation where we felt there was nowhere else to go with the problem!! I think the Secretary possibly realised how upset we both were as she called back the same day and stated that the Cardiologist had now viewed the scan and that the structure of the heart was all good and the problems with the face swelling and breathing problems were probably due to Arrhythmia. That made us both happy, for a while at least. He prescribed me some different medication for the Arrhythmia and I was to stay on the Anti-Coagulants. The Beta Blockers were to stop. A follow up telephone consult was to be conducted in about a month's time.

The Covid 19 situation was beginning to alleviate slightly, with the Government easing some restrictions on certain businesses at the beginning of June, with more shops, gyms and other professions to be re-opened in July. This was too much relief of the majority of the population, but some people were still being slightly mindless as to the fact it was still a serious pandemic, and they were gathering in large groups and ignoring guidelines to still stay vigilant. The weather was being very kind, and the Beaches were packed, meaning that social distancing had gone completely out of the window. The number of people dying had now surpassed 40,000 and the NHS was still under enormous pressure, but death rates and transmission rates were falling.

People were starting to book holidays again, and I must admit we actually booked a Camping trip, only to have it cancelled a few days later. At this point we decided not to bother booking anything until this was all over.

Little did we know at the time it was going to be a very, very long Wait.

At this point I had not taken any days off from my job in years, mainly because I love what I do and was very seldom unwell, but I was finding it harder to perform my duties and was even finding it hard to climb the stairs at home and perform simple tasks like housework and cooking. Needless to say I was now, having to take the odd day off from work which really annoyed me. Even though I had started on different medication from the Cardiologist, the problem was not getting any better and if anything it was getting worse. I was just wishing someone would get to the root of my problem.

I woke up one morning and looked in the mirror, not a pretty sight at the best of times, but OMG I could not believe what I saw!!! I looked like I had gone 12 rounds with a Boxer. My face was so swollen and looked like it would explode, and my eyes were like slats in the snow. It was not a pleasant vision believe me. Tim was horrified when he saw me and advised me to take a couple of selfies to show anyone who wanted to see them. My God they were bad photos. I phoned the Doctors and Hallelujah!!! They agreed it was at last time for me to see someone face to face.

Enter the kindest loveliest Clinician called Amanda, and for the first time I felt that someone was actually listening to me. I showed her the photos and she was horrified (I wasn't too chuffed myself). I explained that my face and neck swelling was happening on standing, bending, walking, and any slight movement. It was suggested that the problem could be the Anti-Coagulants, but they would need to contact the Cardiologist to find out for sure and work out what to do next. On leaving the practice, she saw my face and neck swelling up, and you could physically see she was concerned. She immediately signed me off work for a week and was going to chase up the Cardiologist.

She called me the next day to see how I was as she was really worried. I had to admit I felt lousy and I was troubled that they had not heard back from the Cardio man. I did suggest that it may be a good idea to repeat the bloods. As they had been done pre-medication, I thought it may be a good idea to do them post-medication to see if there was anything in the bloods that may show up what was causing the problem. She totally agreed and the bloods were done that day. I was advised to call on the Friday to get the results.

I called on the Friday anticipating the results only to be told that the Doctor had not had a chance to look at them and had gone home!!! I spoke to a different Clinician but she couldn't give me the results as it needed to be the Doctor, but she did mention that something was slightly raised (again?) but didn't elaborate any further. I really wish she hadn't said anything at this point as that was a little worrying. She made me an appointment to speak via the phone with the Doctor on the Monday. As you can imagine the weekend was unpleasantly long. Things were getting more displeasing and it was just so frustrating when you know something is wrong and it just looks like no-one is listening. My medication had been changed so many times that it appeared to me that the drugs were not working and this needed investigating a lot further. It seemed like this had been going on for ages and we were getting no-where apart from me getting worse day by day.

MONDAY 6th JULY, A DAY TO REMEMBER.

After what seemed like a very long weekend, Monday arrived, and the Doctor called. She asked me to send over the photos which I did. Again, it was mentioned that something was slightly raised on my bloods but yet again this was not elaborated on. She asked what seemed to be a lot of questions, and it was at this point I lost the plot!!! I broke down crying and begged her to do something to help me. I really felt like I couldn't go on like this. She said she had to make a few calls and would get back to me, which in fairness she promptly did. She informed me that I had to go straight to the Ambulatory Care Department at the local Hospital. At last something was happening but boy was I worried, as was Tim.

Feeling very anxious and stressed, we took ourselves off to the Hospital. I was worried even more by the fact that Tim would not be able to come in with me as I didn't feel well enough to cope with this on my own, but when we arrived at the hospital my breathing got worse and I nearly fainted. The team that were checking people at the door were amazing and fetched a wheelchair for me straight away, and at this point they also agreed that Tim could wheel me down to Ambulatory Care. What a bonus!!! Our temperatures were checked, hands sanitised, masks on and off we went. On arrival at the unit, they agreed that Tim could stay with me. What a relief that was.

Bloods were taken, temperature was taken again, blood pressure checked which was high, but I wasn't surprised considering how stressed I was, and an ECG performed and then off to x ray. On returning from the X-ray department, I was examined by a lovely young

Doctor, and I must admit it was nice to see someone face to face and he was really caring and listening to what I was saying. He explained that something was raised on the blood result which was inflammation. Now I knew, but I was none the wiser.

He arranged for a CT scan to be performed, and he explained there would be about a 2 and a half hour wait, in which time I could not eat anything, which was poop because I was starving!!! The wait seemed to go on for ever.

Eventually we arrived at the CT scan area where a Cannula was placed in my arm. It was explained to me that a liquid would be put into the Cannula which would make me feel warm and give me the feeling as if I had wet myself!!! They said this was perfectly normal. Not in my book it wasn't!! The scan only took about 5 minutes, and yes, I had the feeling like I had wet myself. A very odd feeling! I checked myself and to my relief I hadn't. We were told to go back to Ambulatory Care and the results would be back with the Doctor in about 1 hour. The Nurses in the care unit were amazing as on arrival back they bought us coffee, sandwiches and crisps which were well appreciated. A ham sandwich has never tasted so good.

We waited patiently for the results hoping to get some answers to the problem. Neither of us were prepared for what was about to happen next.

Chapter 5

Cancer.

STRESSFUL DAYS.
SMACK.

"We have found a Mass in the Right Lung, And Suspect its Cancer".

There, I said it. The Doctor said it was based on the Radiologists report. The words rang around in my ears and Tim and I just looked at each other in utter shock and bewilderment. We both had a little trouble understanding what was going on, as I had not had any obvious signs of Lung Cancer, and two and a half months ago the bloods and X-rays were fine. I knew I was poorly, but this was ridiculous!!!

The Doctor explained that the mass was in what was called the Hilar region of the Lung, and that the cause of all my problems was that it was pressing on what is called the Superior Vena Cava, which is the main vein in the body that controls the flow of blood from the head, neck, arms and chest to the Heart, and it was this that was causing the breathing problems and the facial swelling. It all sounded very frightening, and I have since learned that it is very rare and serious.

He advised us that Chemotherapy and/or Radiology would probably happen (Brain overload) and that he would refer me onto the team that would deal with this.

I think at this point there should have been a million and one questions, but there just wasn't. Just shock and lots of hugs! Back to the waiting room, the Cannula was removed, and the Doctor informed us he would call the next day. We walked home in silence and numb.

So, where to begin! Couldn't be, could it? Can't be, possibly is? Thinking the worst, thinking the best? Is it just a bad dream? Not real? Didn't know what to think!

On arriving home, there were a lot of hugs, but no tears. We decided, as we always do, to try and put a positive stance on the situation and stay strong. This was not going to be easy to do, but it is the way we always dealt with things and we were not going to change now!!! At least we had a rough idea of what the problem was, and obviously it wasn't the outcome we wanted, but we were still not entirely sure of what we were dealing with and decided to put all our faith in the Medical Team.

It was hard to know what to do next, so rightly or wrongly we decided to let family, close friends and the Management at work know what was going on. Is there a right or wrong in these situations? I think it's a personal choice, and it may not be right for everyone, but this decision was ours.

My Dad was the hardest to tell, as he had been through this with my Mum when she had Cancer. His response was what I expected. Bless him, he can be a bit of a doom and gloom merchant! But by the end of the call, and us trying to put a positive outlook on things, he seemed to be a little more comfortable with the situation, although I suspect he probably wasn't.

Everyone else seemed to be very sympathetic and understanding and offered support and love, although I suspect there was a lot for them to take in as well. I explained that I was not going to run away from this and go head on into battle!! "I'VE GOT THIS".

Tim and I talked about everything from Funerals to Bank Accounts, what to do with the house and all the other important issues some people discuss at a time like this. I know it doesn't sound like a very positive conversation, but to us it was. These are all important concerns to discuss and the situation seemed to prompt us talking about these matters sooner rather than later. Apparently, 99% of newly diagnosed Cancer patients make arranging their funeral the number one priority. I fell into this way of thinking, but a few days later when I tried to make the call to the Funeral Directors, I just couldn't go through with it. I was not ready for that yet. I can't really remember much about the rest of the evening, and to be honest this was going to be a long night. I tossed and turned all night, and didn't get much sleep and I was so grateful and relieved when the morning finally came.

The next day started with what was to turn out to be a very long frustrating 2 weeks. It was explained to me that I would be put on what they call a 2-week pathway where I should be seen by someone within 2 weeks. We heard nothing for the next two days which sort of messes with your head as all you want to know is that something is going to happen. I realise that sounds like I'm being impatient but given the situation I'm sure you understand.

However, 5 days later, on the Friday I was informed that a CT scan had been booked for the following Tuesday to see if the Cancer had spread anywhere else, and in their ultimate wisdom, on the same day, they booked a Bronchoscopy and Biopsy, a procedure where they put a thin tube up through the Nose, down to the Lung and they can remove a piece of the Cancer for analysis. This was going to be a long day, but at least things were happening.

I had to go back to Ambulatory Care for a Covid test, which by now was my third. Things seemed to be getting even worse for me to the point I could hardly walk without struggling to breathe, but things were finally moving forward now.

After what seemed to be another very long weekend, we got to Tuesday and prepared for a long day. I had to be sedated for the Bronchoscopy and Biopsy, but I think I went out completely as I didn't remember anything about it. The Surgeon also put me a high dose of Steroids as this would help with my breathing. The problem was, he didn't make any notes on my records about the Steroids which would prove problematic further down the line. Off for the CT scan and we were done. Now the waiting games begin.

We got to the Friday teatime and hadn't heard anything. This was going to be yet another long weekend!!! The lack of communication was starting to feel intolerable and caused us both very high levels of tension and anxiety. If you didn't feel ill already you soon would!!! Another stressful few days!

Tim had to go into work on the Monday, and I was feeling a little better. I think this may have been down to the Steroids. I decided to try a little housework, just slowly and gently, but this proved not to be one of my best ideas, as I put myself completely down in my boots and had to take a daytime nap. When I eventually woke up I felt like crap. Tim had arrived home from work by now and was worried about my condition, checking my blood pressure and Heart rate regularly as we had our own monitor to do so. They were completely off the scale. He was going to call 999 but I persuaded him to call 111 instead. I didn't want to be a pain to anyone, something further down line I realised I would have to be. He called 111 and explained everything and they advised us to go to A&E, but we had to spell out to them that we couldn't due to not being able to walk and breathe properly. They sent a Paramedic who was amazing.

He checked everything and decided that I didn't need to go to the hospital as they would only repeat what he had done, and he was more than happy with what he had seen. He did explain that I had severe fatigue, probably due to the decrease in Steroids, topped with more stress and anxiety and to call the Doctors the next day and be a pain in the 'butt' (not chasing this time) to get some answers as to where we were moving forward.

FRUSTRATION.

It had now been over 3 weeks since diagnosis, and nothing since. No results, no communication, just nothing. So much for the 2-week pathway!

The next day I spoke to the Doctors and they were horrified that I hadn't heard anything and vowed to chase things up immediately. In fairness to them, they called straight back and informed me the case had been referred to the MDT team (Medical Disciplinary Team) and they were discussing my case the next day (Wednesday) and someone would get back to me.

After what seemed again another long day, the call finally came through at 5pm. It was from the dedicated Cancer Nurse specialist who was to be my key worker. I must admit, what she told us had left us both feeling a little numb and not overly positive.

The mass in the Lung was extensive and possibly malignant (possibly?) leaving no doubt it was Lung Cancer. They had put an extensive plan in place for me. 1. Stent to be inserted to ease swelling and breathing. 2. A PET scan. (Positron Emission Tomography) 3. A second more extensive biopsy. 4. Results then start treatment.

There was a lot to take in here, but at least someone had informed us as to what was going on and something at last was going to happen. This was going to be a long journey, but one we were both going to embrace. I had to increase my Steroids again as well. I had not been sleeping that well since I had started the Steroids, and the Nurse was horrified when I told her I was taking them morning and evening. Steroids cause insomnia!!! She advised me to take them morning and lunchtime. Again, a lack of communication! She advised me she would call back the next day with a plan of action. The call did leave us a bit numb, but we decided to try and stay as positive and upbeat as we could, and try not to look for negatives, a little hard giving the situation.

I went off to bed that night expecting another bad night's sleep, and oh my God, the pain in my chest was horrendous. It was really bad. I tried to convince myself it was heartburn or indigestion. It just didn't feel right at all. So I called out for Tim. I crawled out of bed and nearly fainted much to his horror. He was going to call 999 but managed to get me down the stairs and the pain seemed to subside a little.

He managed to get me comfortable, and the pain eased even more. Stress and anxiety can be a funny thing, but this wasn't funny. With the pain subsiding, I went back off to bed and managed a little sleep, albeit broken.

The Cancer Nurse called the next day to say that the Stent insertion had been booked in 4 days' time on Monday 27th July and that I would need to have another Covid test prior to the procedure. Also, the PET scan was booked two days after the Stent being put in place. It was going to be a busy week, but I wasn't complaining!! Tim explained to her what had happened the night before, and she advised us to go straight to Ambulatory

Care as she wanted my Heart checked. She also explained how she was appalled as it seemed we had 'lost' 2 weeks due to a lack of communication. Not what we wanted to hear given the situation. She did hint towards "there is going to be trouble", not an actual quote but hopefully you get the gist of it. So off we went again, Covid test and more bloods, X-ray's and an ECG. The bloods were all good, no change in the X-ray from previously, and the ECG was fine. We did ask if the Biopsy results were back as we had not received them, and we were told that they were inconclusive as the surgeon could not get to the area he wanted to. Thought that was a little odd? Also, the CT scan had revealed, much to our relief that the Cancer had not spread anywhere else.

A different Cancer nurse called Sharon came to see me while I was in Ambulatory Care, and she was to become my dedicated Nurse and she was absolutely lovely. She couldn't apologise enough for all the problems, a point I was getting a little sick of hearing, but you can't get bitter, got to get better. I was still getting a little pain in the right-hand side of my chest, but had put it, rightly or wrongly, down to a pulled muscle as I had mentioned it on several occasions to the Doctors and they were not concerned. She explained that it was probably Cancer pain, so she prescribed me Morphine!!!! I was horrified at this, as I had always associated Morphine with end of life care and I sure as hell was not ready for that yet. Got that one wrong! It still messed with my head, but I accepted it.

STENT.

Oh boy, what a day this was!!! We had to be at the Hospital for 7.30am in the morning, and I must admit

I was excited to get this procedure done as I thought it would be my getaway from the swelling and the breathing problems and I had grandeur's of running and carrying on as normal afterwards. A Stent is a small tube that is inserted into a blocked passageway to open it up and restores the flow of the blood, easing the swelling and aiding the breathing, so you can see why I was getting excited!! Tim was allowed to push me to the ward in a wheelchair as I was still having trouble walking and breathing and boy he had a long walk. On arrival at the ward we were met by what I can only describe as a right Jobsworth, who promptly asked me if I had been self-isolating for 14 days. Now as I had only found out 4 days ago about the procedure, I found that a little odd and worrying and she gave me the impression that the procedure may not go ahead. For the first time in this whole journey I cried. Another Nurse came along who was very kind, caring and understanding, and she explained that they only needed to know so they could work out what ward to put me in due to Covid, and that the procedure would go ahead. Phew, what a relief, but someone really needed to have a word with Jobsworth!!

I said goodbye to Tim and the Nurse wheeled me off to the ward. She went through all the paperwork with me and asked a lot of questions. She took my temperature and blood pressure, and all of the other pre-op checks that were needed and I settled in feeling happy again. In stepped the Anaesthetist.

To say he didn't fill me with confidence was not an exaggeration. He was whittling on about numbing the back of the spine? I did feel at this time obliged to 'butt' in and explain I was having a stent fitted, to which he replied, "oh, give me a minute, I need to read the notes properly".

My general demeanour was starting to fail me somewhat. The Anaesthetist came back and explained that he was concerned about my breathing, and that I would be whisked straight off to ICU (Intensive Care Unit) for monitoring after the Stent had been inserted. Enter the Surgeon. On the surface of it she seemed lovely, but boy did she freak me out to beyond comprehension. She explained it was a very dangerous procedure that could have a lot of complications, one being that a blood clot could go into the Heart and I would have to be 'blue lighted' to London. So now I was beyond scared yet again. She gave me some paperwork to sign for the Surgery, and promptly asked me to phone Tim to get him to come back to the hospital straight away she could talk to us together. That put my stress levels through the roof and obviously I was thinking the worst.

What Tim must have thought I can't even imagine.

As Tim was over half an hour away from the Hospital it was going to be a long wait. I signed the paperwork as I felt I really didn't have much choice.

I took myself of to the bathroom, looked in the mirror, and said to myself "you're fucked". Please excuse me for being so candid, but that was exactly how I felt. I have faced some low points in my life, but I honestly think this was as low as it could go.

Tim eventually arrived back at the hospital, and we were put in a side ward to talk about what had happened. I tried as best as I could to explain, but I was so upset it probably came out as 'gobbledygook'!! In a moment of pure madness, I did say to Tim that I felt like giving up, and at that point I genuinely did. Tim was great and snapped me out of it and in his immortal words he said to me, "We have not come this far too only come this far". He's great with words, and it did the job.

The Surgeon came into the room, and for some reason the conversation seemed different? She explained everything to Tim and it sounded poles apart from what I had heard. Maybe it was just me not listening properly, but I was on my own and in a bit of a state when the initial discussion took place. Tim asked if she had done many of the procedures before and she said she had done a lot and all with good outcomes. If only she had said that earlier, or maybe I should have asked. I started to feel that maybe, just maybe this was going to be alright.

Tim and I hugged, off he went home again, and it was all systems go.

Off to theatre we went, and I distinctly remember the Anaesthetist trying to shove things up my nose and then I was asleep. I remember waking up and shouting "Timmy, Timmy, I'm alive I'm alive"! What the hell the Theatre team must have thought I have no idea but I'm sure (and hope) they have heard worse, and you better believe it when I say I was overjoyed and grateful to be alive.

I was taken off to ICU where I would spend the next 24 hours. I was groggy for a while but apart from that all was good. The strangest thing was, I could breathe normally and my face was not puffy. I took a selfie and couldn't believe what I saw. I was very happy. I managed to speak to Tim who, quite rightly was overjoyed. The team in ICU were amazing. Nothing was too much trouble for them, and their dedication was magnificent. I could not praise them enough.

So, after a bad night's sleep, it was time to go home and I just could not wait. Tim came and collected me, and we were off!! We stopped at a well-known drive through food outlet, and Tim bought me a Strawberry Milkshake. I can honestly say, a £1000 bottle of Champagne would not have tasted better. It was heaven. Tim was laughing at me as I must have looked like a little kid, but boy, I enjoyed it.

PET SCAN AND EBUS
(Echo Bronchial Ultra-Sound)

Two days later we were of again for the PET scan. This is the long tunnel thing that we have all seen and under normal circumstances, I think I would have panicked about it, as a lot of people do but given what had happened on Monday, this was going to be a walk in the park. They pump you with radioactive material, then you wait an hour and then it takes about 20 minutes for the procedure, which seems a long time when you're confined in a tunnel. I was so tired that I don't really remember too much about it, apart from being glad when it was over.

The Cancer Nurse called a few days later and explained that the results were in. They had found what they wanted and it looked at that point like it may have spread to the Lymph Nodes. It was important to start treatment as soon as possible so I could at least try and get back to some sort of normality and possibly return to work and training. I found that a little odd given the circumstances and the way I was feeling but it did fill us with some sort of positivity. She also said that the EBUS procedure would be booked in about 2 weeks' time as they wanted to move things along. I did point out to her that this had gone on long enough and begged her to try and get it done sooner. Bless her, she made a call and it was all booked for the following week, which was a great relief to Tim and me. She also mentioned that when the results were in there would be a plan put in place for treatment going forward, and she even made reference for a three to six month plan to get me back to work. Again this all sounded very positive, but sadly this was not to be.

I was booked for the EBUS the following week on Thursday 6th August, whereby another Biopsy would be taken, sent to Birmingham for Molecular testing and then they could work out the best course of treatment for me. I saw this as the last of the invasive procedures. Wrong again!!

After another Covid test (number 9) we arrived at the hospital for the EBUS. The Surgeon went through all the 'dodgy' bits and said there was nothing to worry about. He was confident that all would be good. I was happy with this. WRONG!!!!

I think I woke up just at the end of the procedure, as I seem to remember a lot of pressure on my chest. This abated very quickly, and I asked the Surgeon if he had managed to get what he needed, and he informed me that all was well and yes, he had. WRONG AGAIN!!

We travelled home via the food outlet again, another milkshake for me. Total heaven once more!

About 6pm that evening, I noticed a slight cough and my lungs which felt a little crackly-like, but we put it down to the procedure I had been through, which you would expect? I tried to settle down for the night, but the crackling seemed to get worse. Somehow it just didn't seem right.

At 9pm Tim suggested we go to A&E as it was getting worse, and I was starting to feel quite ill. Always best to get things checked if you're worried and as it turned out it was just as well we did.

I could not believe how busy A&E was. Because of the Covid situation, we decided to wait outside as I didn't feel safe inside due to the volume of people, but I must admit some of them didn't seem like they really needed to be there. We heard a lot of shouting and swearing, and people making their voices known as to how long they had been waiting and they were not happy. This was so unfair on the team that was working. They really didn't deserve to be treated like that. Some people just needed to realise that they were doing their job to the best of their ability, and to show them the respect they thoroughly deserved.

With what seemed like a forever wait, eventually I had Bloods taken and an X-ray, and then it was back outside away from the madness. We had now been in A&E for 4 hours, and the crackling was getting worse, and I was also in pain as I had missed my pain killers. To be honest I just wanted to go home. Tim explained the situation to the Nurse and she kindly put me in a side room and fetched me some pain killers. I really appreciated what she done and was grateful for her act of kindness.

The Doctor eventually came to see me and explained that I had a serious infection and would need Intravenous Anti-Biotics immediately and a Saline drip as I was dehydrated. Tim had gone home by now as he wasn't allowed in due to Covid, so I text and informed him of what was happening.

Another Doctor came to see me and explained that the infection was very, very serious and that it was called Aspiration Pneumonia and that part of my right hand Lung had collapsed. This had been caused by the EBUS but he said there was nothing to worry about!!! Easy for him to say!

I couldn't help thinking what could go wrong next, and yes, I was worried. I was to be admitted to a Ward until the infection had cleared up. I didn't have a problem with this as I felt so rough and just wanted to feel better.

I eventually arrived on the Ward, only to be told it was the old and frail Dementia Ward. The way I was feeling I was going to fit in well! The Nurses were amazing, and I could not believe the care and attention given to the patients. I did feel a little guilty as I was feeling a little uncomfortable being there, but I needn't have worried. It was a very eye-opening experience.

The plan was to stay overnight, be pumped with Anti-Biotics, Bloods taken in the morning and if all was OK I could go home. In the meantime, Tim had to prepare an overnight bag and drop it off at the Hospital. I think he must have put everything in it apart from the Kitchen Sink, and the poor Nurse that bought it me was really struggling to lift it, but he done a great job, and I didn't want for anything.

The Bloods were taken the next morning, and sadly the infection was still bad, so it was going to be another overnight stay. Now as much as I wanted to go home, I knew I was in the right place and was happy to stay until all was well. I had a visit from a lovely Egyptian Respiratory Consultant whose name we couldn't pronounce, but it started with an M so for whatever reason only know to us, we decided to call Dr MooMoo. He again explained that part of the right Lung had collapsed but they were not overly concerned about that. I bloody well was!!! He had also made me a follow up appointment 5 days later to see him. I was to go home the next day.

AND THE NEXT PROBLEM IS;

So, after a broken night's sleep and waiting what seemed an eternity for a bag full of Medication I was released. But just before we move on, I just have to say again how amazing all of the Hospital team are, and that includes everyone. They really go above and beyond their duties to care for their patients. And as far as the food, WOW!!! They've got that right!!! And they don't hold back on the portions either, Yummy.

The next few days seemed OK, but I was just oh so tired all the time, randomly falling asleep, and so lethargic. My breathing wasn't great and I was finding it hard just to stand up. I found myself having to crawl up the stairs, and thirsty, OMG, I just could not find anything to quench my thirst. Didn't matter what I drank, I was still parched. I had a bad case of 'cotton mouth' constantly. As a result of drinking so much, I was weeing for England, having to go to the toilet a hideous amount of times a night.

Having a downstairs toilet was causing me problems as getting up and down the stairs was such a task and trying to tackle that five to six times in the night was not funny. Enter Tim with a 'light-bulb' moment. Now in the past we had spent a lot of time Camping, a pursuit we both loved and embraced. We tended to go to more quiet Campsites with the minimum of facilities as they were normally a lot more discreet. Heaven! Consequently, we had all our own equipment including a portable toilet. I think we can all see where this one is going. So yes, it was placed in the Bedroom and my problem was sorted. We affectionately called the toilet my Potty!!! If it had not been for that I probably would have been confined to the downstairs sofa, and as comfortable as it was, I really didn't fancy it much.

The thirst was getting worse, as was my lethargy, so two days later I called Sharon the Cancer Nurse to inform her. I really couldn't stand much more. She arranged for me to go over to the Hospital again as she was concerned about my Blood sugar levels. So off we went again, and just when you thought nothing else could go wrong, I was informed I had Steroid induced Hyperglycaemia, Diabetes bought on by the Steroids. Apparently, my Blood sugar levels were off the scale completely with the high being 42. It did come to light sometime in the future, that I was moments away from a Diabetic coma. I could have died at any given moment that day!

We were taken back to, yes you've guessed it Ambulatory Care for more Bloods and tests. I was given a shot of Insulin and given Medication to go home with when I was ready to leave. The team in the department were really worried as my levels remained very high, and they called Dr MooMoo. He came and told me there was nothing to worry about but given what came to light I think I had every right to be worried AGAIN!!! He sent me home with the medication. It had also been arranged for Tim to meet someone outside of the Hospital to collect a Glucose monitoring machine. He took me home first and then went back to collect it. Things started to go a little pear shaped for him, as the Diabetic Nurse that gave him the machine was very angry and she thought that I was on the wrong dose of medication. When Tim got home, to say he was not very happy was not an exaggeration. We had to phone Ambulatory Care again and he was informed to go the Hospital Pharmacy to get the Medication changed. This was not his favourite place as he had been there on several occasions and he referred to it as the Dungeon being run by Jobsworth's. Not like your everyday normal Pharmacy. So, off he toddled, only to be met there by Dr MooMoo who was very angry that someone had interfered with the Medication. He wasn't angry with Tim, and may I suggest at this point it was just as well he wasn't, but at someone else for interfering. Dr MooMoo said the Medication was correct, so Tim came home, less than impressed.

My Steroids were reduced, and I was informed it would take a few days to start to feel better, but all would be fine. If only that had been true! Over the weekend the thirst was worse, my blood sugars were not coming down and the lethargy was getting worse. I just couldn't stay awake. I felt awful. Sharon called me on the Monday and I just broke down in tears and couldn't talk to her so Tim had to inform her of what had been going on. She said she would talk too Dr MooMoo and get back to us as she seemed to think I would need my Medication increased. When she got back to us we were horrified to find out that Dr MooMoo had said to stay on the same Medication until Wednesday when he would review it again. We were not overly convinced, especially after what the Diabetic Nurse had said, but we assumed he knew what he was doing and went along with it. Tuesday and Wednesday were horrendous, and things were not getting any better so when Sharon called, she said she would speak to Doctor MooMoo again. UREKA!!! He agreed to double the Medication, though why he couldn't have done that Monday was beyond our comprehension. I was still very sleepy on the Thursday but by the Friday things had improved immensely. For the first time in weeks I felt awake. My sugar levels were lower, not by much, but they were going in the right direction, and for the first time in ages, we had a good weekend.

If I said my Journey so far has been a Roller Coaster that would be an understatement. Technically if it could have gone wrong it probably had. We have experienced very up and down moments, tears and laughter, but it's a Journey you can learn from. It would be all too easy to get very angry about a lot of situations, but that takes up too much energy, and the main thing is to focus on staying positive and trying to stay abreast of the situation. "We are in this together".

Sharon the Cancer Nurse called a few days later and confirmed that I had Non-Small Cell Lung Cancer and they thought it had spread to the Lymph Nodes. At least we now knew. She said again that the samples were being sent to Birmingham for Molecular testing and a plan of treatment would be put in place for me. She also said it was not curable but treatable, and I would receive an appointment with the Oncologist once a plan was in place. It had now been six weeks since the initial diagnosis.

There are two different types of Lung Cancer, Non-Small Cell and Small Cell. Apparently if you are going to get one, the Non-Small Cell Cancer is the better one to have, which was mine. Not much comfort but I took that as more positive than negative. A small mercy that we were grateful for given the circumstances!

We received a letter on the 22nd August confirming that the results were in and that I was to see the Oncologist four days later.

Although we were both pleased that at least we would soon know what we were going to have to deal with, I must admit that now we were going to get some answers

I started to get a little scared as to what was going to be said. We had waited so long to get to this point, but somehow it now seemed more real. I fully understood that going forward would not be pleasant, and I guess I worried about it being good or bad news, and not knowing how long I had. That was the worst thought. We decided to meet this head on and stay strong and positive throughout.

The next few days seemed to drag by, with me constantly falling asleep. I did have moments of being awake, and feeling quite good but they seemed few and far between.

For years I had been cutting Tim's hair, and in a moment of madness I offered to do it for him as I felt quite good and thought I could cope with doing it. He wasn't too keen at first, as I think he was worried that I might mess it up, but I assured him I was fine. So, in I went with the Clippers. I was concerned about standing for a longish length of time, but decided if I took several rests, I should be alright. I was impressed at how I managed and was coping well until the final bit when my hand started to shake. Now I don't know if it was the vibration of the Clippers or I was tired, but it didn't feel good. I only had to do around the ears!!! But BOOM!! I survived it, and I must admit I done a pretty good job, and I think Tim was pleased as well as relieved. As was I!!!

I was trying as hard as possible to carry on as normal, but it seemed to me 'normal' disappeared months ago. I was still constantly falling asleep but decided if my body needed sleep then it could have it. My Blood sugars were still a little all over the place which could have been the cause, but after doing some research it might possibly have been the Cancer that was causing the fatigue. Either way I was tired. I had also developed a nasty cough which felt like a tickle in the throat but seemed to be getting worse. It wasn't there all the time but would come and go. Again, we put it down to the Cancer. The next day the cough seemed no better and had a slight tinge of Blood in it which slightly concerned Tim, but again he researched it and was happy enough.

It sometimes feels hard to get to talk to anyone if you have a problem, as you know everyone is busy and you don't want to be a pain in the 'butt'. It's just something you learn very quickly you have to be. Don't get me wrong, there are PLENTY of advice lines, but you do need to ask for help even if you think your being a nuisance. That's what they are there for. Doing your own research helps but beware, it can throw up good and sometimes bad. Always use trusted UK websites and check the dates. Some Data goes back years and could be out of date at the time off looking as things move forward quite quickly now with new treatments and updates being added all of the time. I found the Macmillan website to be exceptionally good.

I managed to speak to Sharon the Cancer Nurse to inform her of the Oncologist Appointment, which she was over the moon to hear, and said that she would be there with me. I also said that Tim would HAVE to be with me as I was not going to go through this on my own. My biggest concern was that due to Covid, patients were not allowed to be accompanied at appointments. In my eyes, and dealing with what was coming, Tim not being there was not an option. I shouldn't have worried as she said it was important that we be there together, and I must admit I was relieved to hear that.

The Oncologist appointment was tomorrow, and we were both feeling a little sceptical about it. I suppose it's the fear of going into the unknown. We know I have Cancer, there's no getting away from that one, but it's the uncertainty that's the scary part. Not knowing how long I would have was playing heavily on my mind as I suppose it would be with anyone in the same situation. We decided again to stay strong and positive and be very open and honest at ALL times with each other, and not hide any feelings. It is important not to face something like this alone.

I must admit, like I said before, I knew this was not going to be a pleasant Journey, but there was a part of me that wanted to know what was going on and if treatment was an option I couldn't wait to get started and hopefully, fingers crossed start to feel well again.

"BRING IT ON"

JUDGEMENT DAY.

On a sunny warm Wednesday morning on the 26th August 2020, we awoke early to prepare ourselves for the day ahead. We were both a little dubious and dare I say a little apprehensive, but as always, we were determined to embrace the day with strength and positivity. Sharon the Cancer Nurse had agreed to meet us there and be in on the Consultation, which really was going to help as we had built up quite a rapport with her by now. Although I still didn't feel great, I managed to wear some normal clothes and put some make up on. I didn't look to bad even if I do say so myself. And for some strange reason, I didn't feel so tired, but that could be put down to anxiety and adrenaline.

We arrived at the Hospital in plenty of time, and I actually managed to walk to the Oncology department unaided, a feat that I was determined I was going to do. Not that there's anything wrong with being wheeled in a Wheelchair, but for my own sanity I needed to walk. We were met by Sharon who was shocked at how well I looked. She said she was so pleased to see me as she didn't think I was going to be well or strong enough to make the appointment. She also said that she was still a little worried about the Diabetes, and she re-iterated how close I was to being in a Diabetic coma and possibly close to death. Not really what you wanted to hear when you're just going to see the Oncologist!! She also admitted that if it could have gone wrong it had. Like I didn't already know that!

Into the Consult room we went where we were met by the Oncologist Dr Cominos. I must admit at this point the fatigue and tiredness kicked in and brain fog appeared. Talk about timing, but at least Tim and Sharon were there as backup. Dr Cominos seemed really nice and she started by asking me a lot of questions about the tiredness and the Diabetes, and as luck had it I had taken the Diabetes monitoring booklet with me. She was concerned that they were still on the high side, and she advised seeing a Diabetic Nurse which Sharon would arrange for me. She also wanted me to wean off the Steroids, but if I started to feel worse again then to resume them.

So the verdict! It was stage 4 Lung Cancer and advanced. Now at this point we should have asked what this meant but we didn't. I think we were both just sitting there numb at what had been said, and it sounded really serious which it was. She explained that the best course of treatment for me was a double dose of Chemotherapy as well as Immunotherapy, a fairly new drug that was having great results. She also said that the treatment was very, very aggressive with a lot of side effects which she did rattle through but to be honest I have no idea what she said and neither did Tim. The biggest concern she had was the other underlying problems that I had, and that I might not be strong enough to take the treatment, and given the way I had been feeling I shared her concerns, but she did say that if it was too much for me they could stop the Chemotherapy at any time. At this point I felt completely out of the game, and as I looked at Tim, I could tell he was feeling the same.

The treatment was to be done every 3 weeks and would be repeated 4 times and then reviewed. This was going to be brutal. I did ask about not having any treatment, though why I said that I don't know, and at that point the Oncologist and Sharon both jumped down my throat (sort of) saying this was really the best thing for me, which actually felt quite positive.

So here we go. The obvious question! How long?

A few months to a year came the answer.

Ouch, that really hurt. A body blow to us both. We both knew this was serious, but maybe not quite that serious.

It felt like someone had hit me with a bolt of lightning. The main statement that rings in your ears is the few months comment but looking back in hindsight this would depend on how I was going to respond to treatment, but she did point out that the Immunotherapy treatment lasted for two years and what a positive comment that was!!! And there was even a mention of going back to work. Another positive! So, if I can stay strong, get the Diabetes under control and take the Chemotherapy I could have a year, or even possibly longer (I didn't hear that bit but thankfully Tim did). As long as my quality of life is good, I will take that. I decided that I wanted to go ahead with the Treatment as I hadn't come this far to give up now and as they said it was the best option for me.

An appointment was to be made for me to start the treatment.

Now I know there should have been a million and one questions we asked but trust me when I say when you're in that kind of situation the brain goes blank. There's a lot of information to take in, and that was for both of us, not just me, and you can't think or function straight. As luck had it Sharon was with us and she was going to do a follow up call in a few days to answer any questions we may have had. She was also going to get a Macmillan Financial Representative to contact us, and arrange for me to see a Diabetic Nurse. She really is an Angel.

The drive home was a little strange as we still really didn't know what to say to each other, but we did stop at the food outlet for a Milkshake but somehow it just didn't taste so good this time round. I think we just needed to get home, sit down, and digest what had been said and get our heads around it all. I had a million and one things running around in my brain, but by the time we arrived home for some reason I started to feel more positive about things. The bottom line being I was going to pass away at some point, and I wanted to get as many Eggs put away in the basket as I could before anything happened. The main thing that kept coming into my head was to sort out a Funeral, but I quickly dismissed this as I had already previously decided not to pursue that. One of the things I wanted to sort were the finances. I had always taken care of them so I needed to go through them with Tim, so he knew what to do. It wasn't that there was a problem with the finances, it was just the job I had always gladly done. We had two Cars, and I didn't think we were going to need both of them, so Tim was to sort out selling one of them.

This caused a dilemma for him as to which one to sell as they were both good Cars!!! We made a list of things to look forward to as well. Christmas, my 60th Birthday in January, and maybe taking a little holiday in the spring! Always got to have something to look forward to!

We informed the rest of the Family, and we told them I was to have 3 months of aggressive Treatment with concerns about me not being strong enough to take it, but the Chemotherapy could stop should I not be able to cope with it, but it was the best course of action for me. At this point we felt there was nothing to be gained by telling them that I may only have 3 months to a year to go. I didn't feel like we were lying to them, just being protective.

We were not expecting treatment to start for a couple of weeks, so this was my chance to try and build up my strength to at least give myself half a chance of coping with the Chemotherapy. Tim and I agreed to remain strong and positive as always and stay upbeat and maintain a sense of Humour!!!!!

We took a call from a Macmillan Representative on the Thursday who explained what financial help we could be entitled to. It was something that we both hadn't really thought about, and it was surprising how much help was out there. This was a relief to us both as we were wondering how we would manage, so it was an avenue worth pursuing. She explained everything in detail and the best part of it was that she would be sorting it all out for us. That was a blessing in disguise as we would not have had a clue where to start. We could not have been more grateful to her.

I was starting to feel a lot better as my Blood Sugars had seemed to sort themselves out and I wasn't feeling as tired and fatigued. Sharon called on the Friday as promised, and it was a positive call. She explained that the Oncologist would not have recommended the Treatment plan unless it was the best for me, and that if I wasn't strong enough, we could alter the program to suit at any time. I was worried that Stage 4 meant that it had spread elsewhere, but Sharon assured me it was localised, being confined to one area. At this point we should have asked for a definition of Stage 4 but we didn't. I have since learned that keeping a pen and paper handy really does come in to its own when needing to ask questions. A trait that I wish I had thought of earlier in the process. She was also very happy with my Blood Sugar levels, and over the moon I was feeling better.

We received the appointment letters from the Hospital and I was to have a pre-assessment done on Monday 31st August, with the first round of treatment to start the following Monday. Things were starting to happen and to be frankly honest, we were both relieved to know at last something was going to be done. As I have previously stated it wasn't going to be pleasant, but with a good mind-set and positive attitude, we were both confident we could get through this, 'TOGETHER'.

The Covid situation was still ongoing, and things had been slowly returning to some sort of normality with restrictions. The rates of infections were lower and not so many people were losing their lives, but sadly some still were. Businesses were going under, but the Government had introduced an EAT OUT TO HELP

OUT scheme whereby you could eat out a lot cheaper to help struggling Restaurants and Pubs. People were taking full advantage of this and who could blame them!!! It had also been suggested that Children return to Schools in September, which I think pleased a lot of adults, but left some people concerned about Covid spreading again.

THE HORSE.

Although we were going through what some might say was a rough time, we still had the Horse to look after. It wasn't easy as I was struggling to walk and breathe and Horses do take a lot of looking after. However, it was an exceptionally good summer and as luck had it, he was able to live out in the field 24 hours a day. One of the other Ladies at the Yard had been helping us with him, which was such a blessing. She really was in love with him and was only too glad to help. She was even riding him a little which was no mean feat as she was nearly 70!!!! I was alright going to the Yard with Tim to start with, but was struggling more and more, and couldn't get to see 'Boy' as much as I wanted to, a situation that was breaking my heart but there was nothing I could do about it. Tim was building quite a rapport with him, which I saw first-hand on one of my few visits. It was heart-warming to see, and I knew the 'Boy' was in good hands.

We had spoken about the long-term plan for him going forward. We knew at some point we were going to have to make a very difficult decision. He was having trouble walking due to severe Arthritis, and the Vet had already alluded to him really struggling through another winter. He had been hindered with his walking the previous winter, we had managed it well, but we were both worried about the winter to come. We just didn't think he would cope with it. We decided that once the winter kicked in it would be time to let him go. I was not going to see him suffer and be in pain just to keep myself happy. We both knew it was not going to be an easy decision but trust me when I say we had his best interest and welfare at heart. I had seen people in the past in the same situation leave things far too long and watched as their Horses were suffering. Not that I would ever blame anyone for leaving it too late. You want to hold onto what's precious for as long as possible. Saying goodbye to a trusted friend is never going to be easy, and it's all down to a personal choice.

On the Friday Tim had to move the 'Boy' back to his old Field. We were lucky in as much as we had spare paddocks, so the Horses could be rotated so as to give the other field's time to rest and the grass to grow. 'Boy' had been grazing in one of the spare ones and the Friday was his day to go back to his old haunt.

I didn't go with Tim on this occasion, but he did say that 'Boy' was mightily happy to be back in his old Field. Now considering his age and Arthritis, I was surprised to hear that he had run around, jumped up in the air and fallen over!!!! But at least I knew he was happy.

On the Saturday morning I took an early call from one of the other Girls from the Yard to say there was a problem with the 'Boy'. He was just lying in the field, couldn't get up and it looked like he had been there a while as he had pooped where he lay. I just went into panic and meltdown mode. Tim jumped straight into action and he was on his way. I was distraught as I couldn't go with him, I was just not strong enough, but I knew he would be in good hands. Tim called me from the Yard to let me know he was still down and just couldn't get up, so I called the Vet as an emergency and she was going to be with him in about 20 minutes.

The Vet arrived and could not really examine him properly as he was down, but she gave him some strong Painkillers to see if that would help him to stand. Sadly, the Painkillers didn't work, and he didn't get up. The Vet seemed to think his back legs had finally given out on him, and there really was not much more that could be done for him. The kindest thing was to put him to sleep. It was almost as if he had taken the decision we had talked about from our hands. Tim and I spoke on the phone for a while and we decided that this would be for the best. I took the call from Tim to say it had been done, and that it was just so peaceful, and that he had just drifted off to sleep. I couldn't believe that my 'Boy' had gone. I was just so upset. I couldn't even be with him in his final moments. That was hard. However, Tim did say given my situation, and the circumstances with the 'Boy' it was probably for the best I wasn't. I had in the meantime arranged for him to be collected by a Cremation Service and requested for his Ashes to be returned to us.

So that was that. We had 21 fabulous Years with the 'Boy', and the memories would last forever. He was hard work at times and could be a little 'sod' when he was younger, but we went on to achieve so much in Competition and had the most pleasurable times with him. He was one of a kind and although he will be sadly missed, he leaves behind the fondest of memories. Thank you, 'Boy'.

PRE-ASSESSMENT
AND 1st TREATMENT.

Monday 31st August arrived and it was off to the Hospital for my pre-assessment for treatment. The Nurse I saw was amazing!!! She took the time to explain everything to me, from the side effect of the treatment, to help lines that would be available should I need them. She also explained to me that I needed to be careful with food. I was to avoid things like Blue Veined Cheeses, Unpasteurised Milk and Cream, all Pro-Biotic Drinks, raw Seafood and under-cooked Meats. Also to avoid Buffets and all you can eat Menus. The reason being these foods can contain a lot of bad bacteria which is not good for you when your Immune system is compromised. I was gutted as one of my favourite foods was Blue Cheese. I did ask about losing my hair, an obvious question, and she explained that my hair would thin out a lot. I had already had my hair cut short in preparation, and to be quite honest with you, losing my hair was not an issue to me. I know it is to most people, but I felt I had more things to worry about than that. And anyway, Tim was ready, armed, and dangerous with the Clippers should I need them!!! My weight, height, blood pressure and temperature were checked as well as another Blood test and an additional Covid test (number 10). As long as the Bloods were alright, treatment could go ahead. I left the Hospital feeling a lot happier with things, although still very apprehensive. My Treatment would start in a weeks' time.

The week was very long, with me just feeling tired and washed out most of the time. I had a wobble during the week and broke down crying. I guess I was just fed up with feeling so rough all the time and the fact I couldn't be with 'Boy' in his final moments got to me, but I don't for one minute suppose it does any harm to let your feelings out every now and then.

Last weekend I thought I had Thrush after checking online for signs and symptoms. Now it's something I had never experienced before so I couldn't be 100% sure but on speaking to Sharon she was convinced that it was and advised me on what to take. I took the treatment for a few days and thing seemed to improve. During the middle of the week I noticed that when I was having a wee it was starting to sting. I spoke to Sharon again and she said it was probably Cystitis. Again it was something I had never had before. She again advised me on what to take. The stinging was getting a lot worse so I decided to call the Doctors on the Friday, only to be met by the 'Receptionist from hell' who said they only had Paramedics on duty and if I really wanted one she would arrange a call back. Your damn right I did as I was in a lot of pain. I did say to her that Tim could collect a Urine pot so someone could check out a wee-wee sample, but she said no one would look at it until the Monday so there was no point. Very helpful!

I took a call from a Practitioner called Viv who was to turn out to be a very important part of my Journey. I explained that I was worried I may have a Urine infection and was concerned as I was going to be starting my treatment on the Monday. She asked me to get Tim to collect a sample pot and she would run a dipstick to see if there was an infection or not. 2 hours wasted thanks to 'the Receptionist from hell'.

Just when you thought nothing else could go wrong, a Urine infection!!!! She prescribed me with Anti-Biotics and a letter to take with me to the hospital on the Monday.

So there lies the other problem. After waiting so long for treatment, I doubted very much it would go ahead given the infection. I called the Cancer unit and spoke to a Nurse who was going to get in touch with the Oncologist, and to turn up on the Monday unless I heard different. I was not holding out a lot of hope.

The weekend was long, and to be honest I felt a little down. I felt fed up with the situation, as it felt like sometimes it was never going to end, and this was about as good as things were going to get. Considering I felt rubbish most of the time, that was a very depressing thought. Tim was my rock as usual, saying it was completely understandable given the situation, and he supplied me with a shoulder to cry on and lots of warm hugs. We did manage to sort a few things out, mainly the Finances. This made me feel a little better as I now knew that should anything happen to me, he would be alright financially and know what to do with payments and anything else that needed sorting as far as the Bank account was concerned. It was very important for us to talk openly and honest about everything, and to discuss issues that I know a lot of people avoid in our situation. Talking about things and putting things in place can give you the peace of mind knowing that you are doing the best you can. This may not work for everyone, but it certainly did for us. Hiding from these conversations does not make them go away but can make things worse in the long run. It's always good to talk.

Monday morning came and I hadn't taken a call from the Cancer unit, but I decided I would call them anyway just to check, and to my utter shock and surprise they said that the treatment was going ahead. BOOM!!! However, 20 minutes later I took another call saying that the treatment would have to be postponed till the Friday. They said that this was down to the fact I had not taken the pre-treatment Steroids and Folic Acid. Apparently I was supposed to start the Steroids the day before I started the Chemotherapy. When I had the appointment with the Oncologist, she had said to me to start Folic Acid immediately, which I did, and that I was to start Steroids after the treatment. So, you can imagine I was very upset and extremely confused. I was told to attend the unit to collect the Medication which I already had? Tim was not happy and when we arrived at the unit it was all I could do to stop him from coming in with me. I asked him to let me try and sort it out myself. When I spoke to the Nurse I explained that I had been taking the Folic Acid, and that I had been told to take the Steroids post treatment. She went off to talk to someone and came back and said they were now happy for treatment to start.

Tim went home happy. More confusion set in when they said that I defiantly should have started the Steroids the day before treatment and they were again not sure if it could go ahead. My thoughts were 'oh no, here we go again. No treatment'. Even at the pre-assessment I had asked about the steroids and was told someone would get back to me. I even called them before the weekend to try and find out but was again told they were sorting it out??? Talk about confusing!!! But it wasn't all doom and gloom. They decided to give me the Steroids there and then, administer the Chemotherapy, and I would have to return on the Tuesday for the Immunotherapy. At last, something was happening.

On the Wednesday my blood sugars were still on the high side, so I called the Cancer unit and was advised to get in touch with the Diabetic Nurse at the Doctors. Apparently one of the side effects of the Chemotherapy I was on can cause Blood Sugars to rise, which given they were on the high side anyway didn't bode too well. I called the Doctors and I got the 'Receptionist from hell' again and she said they could make me an appointment in about a week and a half time!!! I must point out at this time that most of the Receptionists were very good and accommodating, but there's always one and I seemed to get her most of the times I called. I did explain the urgency of the situation, but she said it was the best they could do. I called the Cancer unit and they said it was down to the Doctors to sort it out, so I called the Doctors AGAIN only to be told that someone would call me back. They never did. Most helpful!!! I felt I had no choice but to call Sharon the Cancer Nurse who was absolutely fuming as she had requested an appointment over two weeks ago. She was going to get in touch with the Doctors. I wished her well with that one, and Tim did comment he would have loved to be a Fly on the wall with that conversation!!

I had been taken off the Diabetic Medication a while ago so I took it upon myself to start taking it again. I didn't know if it was the right thing to do but given the situation, I felt I had little choice. I wouldn't recommend anyone else to do this, but I felt it was right for me at the time.

Sharon called the next day and explained that she had got no-where with the Doctors, which didn't surprise me, and that she was arranging for the District Diabetic Nurse to get in touch. In the meantime, someone from the Surgery called and said that the Doctor wanted to me to start back on the Diabetic Medication. This could have been sorted so much earlier, but at least the outcome was at last sorted.

By Thursday I really didn't feel well at all. I was very shivery and felt a bit sick. I took this as normal side effects from the Chemotherapy, but I was also not convinced that the Urine infection was clearing up. One of the things they give you in the Cancer unit is an Anti-Emetic, a drug that stops you feeling sick, so I took one and they do work. A very sleepy day and just felt completely wiped out. I think there may be many more of these days to come.

JUST WHEN YOU THOUGHT IT COULDN'T GET WORSE!!!

Friday! Now this was going to be a day to remember!!! I woke up in the morning, and OMG I just felt like shit. I can't remember ever feeling so rough and seeing as what I had been through recently found that a little hard to understand. I just couldn't get warm, just wanted to sleep and generally felt very, very unwell. My temperature had gone up to 37.7 and on some of the paperwork we had received from the Cancer unit, it had stated that if it went above 37.5, we were to call the unit immediately. Tim called them and after a lot of questions we were advised to go straight to A&E, but given the fact I could not stand without feeling faint, let alone walk to A&E, he was advised to dial 999, which he done. The ambulance arrived within 5 minutes. The Paramedics were just so kind and understanding and very calming. The only thing

I was worried about was the fact I had no knickers on!!!
Because of the Urine infection, I decided not to wear any
knickers at night and being summer I only had a t shirt
and shorts set of pyjamas on. Now I might have been
somewhat out of the game, and feeling like crap, but I
did still hold with some dignity.

The Paramedic's conducted a lot of tests, and they
both agreed I needed to go straight to Hospital as they
suspected I had what they called Urosepsis. Urosepsis is a
term used to describe a type of Sepsis that is caused by
an infection. It is a complication often caused by Urinary
tract infections that are not treated quickly or properly.

That sounded very serious and apparently it was. My
temperature had gone up to 39. My mind was going a
little fuzzy at this point, but I remember saying to the
Paramedics that I just couldn't get warm, but they said I
was that hot to the touch they could fry an egg on my
skin. Still not wearing any knickers, I was taken to hospital
in the Ambulance.

On arrival at the hospital I could not believe how
quickly everyone kicked into gear. They were just
amazing. With Sepsis there is what is known as 'the
Golden hour' whereby treatment is essential within that
time frame, and boy were they on it!!! I had IV Anti-
Biotics and a Saline drip put in my arm straight away,
and Bloods and X-rays were taken immediately. It
appeared that the Urine infection had got worse because
my Immune system was compromised due to the
Chemotherapy. Just to make matters even grimmer my
noo-noo started to sting really badly. I felt like I wanted
to pass water, so was placed on a commode, and oh boy
the pain!!! I couldn't pass anything and it felt like someone
had put a red-hot poker right inside my noo-noo. I think

I can honestly say I had never experienced pain like it before. I was begging for someone to help me as I just couldn't stand it. I am not normally one to make a fuss, but the pain was unbearable. Eventually the Nurse bought me some Morphine and Paracetamol and boy did that help. What a relief.

Everything seemed to settle down and thankfully I started to feel better. Dr MooMoo came to see me and explained that if my temperature had gone down on the Saturday I could go home. I was moved to another ward and this was to be my home for the next 24 hours. Tim bought me another overnight bag full to the brim, and yes, I now had knickers on!!!! I was starting to feel even better, the stinging had stopped, but I was still tired. I still can't believe how wonderful all the team were in the Hospital. They all just acted so quickly, and I think I probably owe them more that I realised.

I had more IV Anti Biotics over night as well as extra medication, so I had a very broken night's sleep, but to be honest, I don't think anyone really sleeps that well in Hospital. I was just grateful that I was feeling better and I knew I was getting the best care there was.

One of the Nurses came to see me on the Saturday morning and explained that Dr MooMoo had said that I was to stay another night as apparently he was coming to see me on the Sunday with a plan?? She couldn't elaborate any more on that, but it was intriguing. A lovely young lady from acute Oncology came to see me and explained that my Bloods were still showing signs of infection, and my temperature was still on the high side so I would have to stay another night anyway. She did say there was no point going home, just too probably be straight back in again. I totally agreed with her, and as much as I wanted to go home, I knew it was the right thing to do. She was an absolute legend. She took the time to talk to me about things, and she listened. She explained that what I was experiencing was a consequence of the Chemotherapy and Immunotherapy and she explained what I could expect moving forward with other side effects and feeling tired and fatigued. She was just so kind and understanding that I could have cried. She put my mind at ease on a lot of things. It was also nice to speak to someone face to face. During this time and because of Covid, most conversations were being done by phone, which I fully understand for safety reasons, but it was just so nice to speak to her.

I didn't sleep well at all again that night, as my cough seemed to be worse and I was up and down like a yoyo weeing all night. I did cough up a small amount of Blood which I alerted the Nurse to and it was noted. In the morning, Dr MooMoo came to see me, and I was waiting in anticipation for his master plan, but he seemed a little angry and asked me "what are you still doing here"!!! He didn't seem to know that I had been told I had to stay anyway because of my temperature and my Bloods still being inaccurate. I said the Nurse had also told me to stay another night as he wanted to see me. I was totally confused by now and he didn't seem too happy. So much for the master plan! He said I could go home with oral Anti-Biotics, and that a Urine sample and Sputum sample would be sent to the lab for analysis and he would call me on Wednesday with the results. I was not going to hold out much hope of that, and yes, you've guessed it, he never did. I could only take that as a sign everything was alright. So I was again released and I must admit it was nice to get home.

For the next few days all I wanted to do was sleep which was explained as being normal due to my treatment by the Acute Oncologist, so I decided to just go with it. Not only that, I still had the stinging in my noo-noo and was weeing for England. I was still on the Anti-Biotics so was in doubt that it was still the infection, but something was going on and it was so painful. By the end of the week, apart from the Urine problem, I started to feel more awake and a lot better.

I even managed to walk about a bit without feeling faint and tackled a Shower which was amazing. The amount of times one stands in the Shower and we just don't think about it and take it for granted, but when that luxury is denied you for whatever reason it makes it feel like you are being Showered with liquid Gold. My hair was starting to thin, but thankfully not coming out in clumps, but as always Tim was poised in anticipation with the Clippers should I need them!!!

With the stinging I was starting to notice a pattern. When it was at its worst, I couldn't pass water properly and it felt like the Urine was trapped in the Urethra. It would come out in small drops and sting like hell when it did. It made me cry and break out in a hot sweat. A cold flannel compress helped a little, but I also noticed that the episode was lasting about one and a half hours. Occasionally it was so bad I had to take Morphine. Also, during the night, I was up about 7-8 times weeing, and sometimes I would also have what I called a stingy episode. Consequently, I was not sleeping well and constantly tired. It was bad enough being wiped out by the Chemotherapy and Immunotherapy treatment, but not being able to sleep due to the wee-wee problem was starting to be intolerable. I called the Doctors on the

Friday to explain to Viv the Clinician what was going on, and she seemed to think it could be down to the Diabetes and suggested another water test. It came back with Blood and Glucose in it, and as I had been off the Diabetic medication again, it was suggested I go back on it and wait for an appointment with the Diabetic Nurse, so I decided this time I was not coming of them until that happened!!! I was really getting fed up with being messed around. It seemed every time they took me off the medication things got worse, and then when I went back on it things got better? The Weekend was quite good, the stinging was still there but I was feeling a lot better in myself, and we even managed to get out of the house for little drive.

On the Monday the Community Diabetic Nurse called at last. To be honest, she was such a treasure, and took the time to explain my type of Diabetes which was now officially called Steroid induced. I was to stay on the medication as this would bring everything under control, and that I should monitor my Bloods three times a day until they were stable. She was certain that this was the way to go, and I was more than grateful for her help and advice. She said she would be in touch on a regular basis to make sure everything was going in the right direction, and true to her word she did.

The next day I done something that made me very, very happy. Housework!! Now I know you think me mad but when you have not been able to do anything for ages, a simple thing like doing some light Housework is such a pleasure!! Again, we go through life doing things without even thinking about them, but when that chore is denied you, it suddenly becomes a luxury to be able to manage it. Things look and feel different! And you notice things in a different way. Things look brighter, and colours and textures seem different when you really look at them. I, like so many never really enjoyed Housework, and I never thought I would get excited about doing it, but I jolly well did!!!!!!

The Oncologist called me on Thursday 24th September, and she stated that despite the concerns she had over me not being able to stand the treatment, she was more than happy with the way things had gone after the first cycle. Despite being in Hospital which was down to the UTI, I was to continue with the treatment as planned. She would be arranging a CT scan in November and would do another follow up appointment early December with the results. That was going to be a long wait but hopefully worth waiting for. I also had my pre-treatment assessment today and all went well and I'm all set for the second round of treatment next week.

True to the acute Oncologists' words, the one that I spoke to when I was in hospital, I have started to feel a lot better over the last few days. I'm not so tired and I've managed to do some things around the house which again makes me very happy. Little pleasures!!! The cough seems a lot better and although the stinging on wee weeing is still there it does seem slightly better. My hair is still thinning but not falling out, and yes, he's still armed and dangerous!!!

SECOND TREATMENT.

The Second treatment went without a hitch, and I managed to get the Steroids right this time, but to be honest I don't feel that it was my fault they were wrong last time. Just down to a lack of communication again. The course of treatment takes about four and a half hours, which is a long time to be sitting around, but you hope in the long run it will do some good so it's worth it. There are various kinds of treatments available and I know that some people can be there all day having theirs, so my time was more than bearable. The Nurses on the unit were amazing again, but they do work so hard. It seems like they are short staffed, but they just get on with it without making any fuss at all. They truly are amazing.

I took another call from the Diabetic Nurse who was more than happy with the way things were going. My Sugar levels were now more stable, and I was to continue with the Diabetic medication, which I was more than happy to do. I also took a welfare call from the local Hospice which completely freaked me out. I had always, and wrongly, associated the Hospice with dying, so imagine my horror when they called. Thankfully I could not have been more wrong. It was explained to me that they were there for help and advice and support in a number of ways, and that if I had any concerns about anything, I could call and just talk to someone, which was lovely to hear. They are there to celebrate and make the most of life, not just for end of life care.

As I was still having trouble with my breathing, they were arranging for a Physio to come and help with my Respiratory problem. This is just one of the amazing services they provide, and I know there are many more.

The next week was a mixture of up and down days, with being wiped out most of the time but having small moments of staying awake, but they were few and far between. Eating became a bit of a problem as my taste buds seemed to have gone AWOL. Everything tastes so bland. Strong flavours were the order of the day. I found strong Lemon Squash perfect for my thirst as well as Salt and Vinegar crisps and the icing on the Cake was Brown Sauce!!! So, it was Brown Sauce on everything!!! Apart from my Breakfast cereal. I had always been an avid Coffee drinker, but now I just couldn't face it, so I turned to lemon Green Tea and put extra Lemon Juice in it and boy did that hit the spot. Also, I just couldn't drink enough Milk in the mornings, having at least three glasses, but when I spoke to the Diabetic Nurse she said it was a good thing, as it provided a lot of Nutrients and Vitamins that were good for me.

I still had the horrible cough, and was coughing up brownish yellowish stuff, which was a bit alarming, and every now and then there would be a bit of Blood in it. I spoke to Sharon the Cancer Nurse about it and she explained it could be what they called Tumour flare. I didn't like the sound of that but she explained that the Tumour can flare up and then shrink due to the Chemo. I liked the sound of that! And when she explained that it means the treatment was working, I liked that even more!!!

My breathing was still quite bad, and I was getting out of breath very easily. I was starting to think that a few of my problems were now starting to be Psychological, as I had been sitting and lying around for ages, all being down to not being able to (or so I thought) do anything, and I could feel myself wasting away. Always having been so fit and active, this was extremely frustrating, but in my mind, I felt I couldn't do anything about it. Again, I was so wrong on this front. After talking to Tim about it, I decided to get up off my 'butt' and do something about it. I needed to get stronger and healthier. I had lost about a stone in Weight, and while some people would be happy with that, in my condition I was not. All my lovely Muscle Mass from Athletics had disappeared and I was gutted about that as well. I knew it wasn't going to be easy, and it would take a lot of effort, but if you change your mind-set and are determined, it's amazing what you can achieve. It's just a case of getting started and staying positive with it.

We were blessed at home with a spare room with a Treadmill and Bike in it so that was going to be my starting point, and I was determined to make it work and I knew Tim would be there to guide and help me so I was in a win-win situation!!!! Not wanting to waste any more time, the next day I was on it. We have a long pathway in our Garden, so I started there. I walked up and down the path 10 times!!! I also managed 2 minute and 30 seconds on the Treadmill and the Bike. I had done all this twice on the same day. Now that may not sound much to you but for me it was a major achievement and boy did it make me feel good. I had at least made start, and now had a foundation to build on. It wasn't going to be easy, but I was determined.

I had been asked by the Diabetic Nurse to call the Doctors and book in for a Diabetic Blood test which I duly done only to be greeted by the 'Receptionist from hell' again. She offered me an appointment 2 days post Chemo treatment, and when I tried to explain to her that I would be completely wiped out and not capable of doing anything she stated she had offered me an appointment and it was up to me whether I took it or not, and that I could always collect a form from the Doctors and have it done at the Hospital. Not most helpful at all as usual. I asked her to get the Clinician I had been dealing with to call me. She huffed a bit and said she would. The Clinician did call me back and she was not too impressed either, but she arranged for me to have the blood test done at the end of that week along with the Flu jab.

There were two Clinicians, Viv and Amanda, that I had been dealing with on a regular basis, and to be honest I trusted them both so much I didn't want to talk to anyone else. They both understood all my problems and they were there for me and nothing was too much trouble. And they listened. Sometimes you can feel that when you are talking to other people, they are nodding their heads but nothing's going in. These two Clinicians really did become my rocks and I will be forever grateful to them both.

The Physio from the Hospice came to the house to see me to help with my breathing, and I can honestly say she was up there with one of the nicest people I think I may have ever met. She gave me some literature on breathing that was relevant to my condition, and a CD with breathing techniques on to listen to. She also took the time to talk me through, and show me some exercises to do which would help. The advice and information was invaluable, and I knew it would assist me going forward. She was also explaining about the fact she was a Buddhist and had just become a Buddhist Nun. I could have spoken to her for hours.

GOOD DAYS BAD DAYS.

Every day through this journey is a learning process. You do get a lot of very valuable information, but there is not a one size fits all guide to what you can expect to experience. You just learn along the way. On several occasions I had to re-order medication from the Doctors.

During the Covid lock-down, the Doctors were taking medication requests by e-mail, which was useful. This stopped once lock-down was eased and they would not be taking requests over the phone and recommended placing the orders by either dropping them off at the Surgery or with the Chemist direct which we done. On one occasion I had put a request in for more medication, and when Tim went to collect it he was told it was not there. He phoned the Surgery and they told him that the Doctors had sent it to the Chemist electronically. So, he called the Chemist again who informed him they had not received it. So, back on the phone to the Doctors again and they said the request had been denied. To say he was not happy was not an exaggeration. He spoke to THE Receptionist from hell again and she told him I would have to speak to the Doctor next week. There was one lot of medication I needed before then, so it was a matter of urgency that I had it. Tim got very assertive with THE Receptionist, not rude, not abusive, but assertive, which he does so well, and in fairness to her she did manage to have a word with the Doctor and she informed Tim that the prescription would be at the chemist in the evening.

He went off to the Chemist in the evening and came back as happy as Larry with a lovely little bag. When I opened it, you can only imagine the look on his face when it was a 'bloody' Sharps Box!!! And no medication! He was not happy. He called the Chemist and they said that the medication was there, so off he went again and eventually, after a lot of phone calls, a long afternoon, and tooing and froing the medication was in the house. I do feel for him sometime, but we got there.

The next few weeks were a combination of good days and bad days again. One day tired, one day not so bad. I was managing to up the times on the Treadmill and Bike to build my strength up, and was actually managing 3 minutes on each. It doesn't sound a lot, but given my situation, and the way I had been feeling, I felt it was a great achievement, and it made me feel good about myself. Little steps!

The Peeing problem was still there intermittently, and on talking to Viv the Clinician at the Doctors they agreed that it couldn't be an infection as it would be there all the time. It was suggested that the problem could have been bought on by the Chemotherapy, which sort of made sense as it started after my first round of Chemo. I was still coughing, but again, it was on and off. Sleeping was starting to be a problem as I was still up weeing about 6-7 times a night. Thank God for the potty!!!!! Because of not sleeping at night I found myself falling asleep a lot during the day which was very frustrating as I felt like I wanted to do things, like the joys of housework, doing exercise and walking out for fresh air. Things that most people would take for granted in everyday life, but for me they were a lifeline of normality, and a joy to achieve. Little pleasures!

Again, the stinging started to get a little worse so I phoned Viv again and she ran another dipstick, and yes you've guessed it, another bloody Urine infection. So back on the Anti-Biotics! This time round I really was starting to feel extremely fed up with the whole situation of not feeling great, and was feeling frustrated as I was hoping to get back to some sort of normality. It was bad enough feeling like crap after Chemo, but having peeing problems was a thing I really could have done without. However, I was only halfway through my treatment, and I knew I just had to be patient. Not one of my better virtues I must add.

As I previously mentioned my weight had seriously dropped, and all of my muscles were gone. That was hard to take as I had been so fit and had good muscle mass. The only way I was going to get this back was to exercise. I really could not afford to lose that much weight.

We decided to up my food intake, healthy of course, to see if that might help, and I was also hoping that it would build my strength up. It did actually seem to work, and the weight went back on a little bit, and I was managing a little more exercise.

I had a letter arrive from the Doctors to arrange an URGENT appointment with them to discuss some Blood results. This made me panic a little, especially the word URGENT. With everything that had gone wrong my mind again went into overdrive, thinking the worst. I called the Doctors and yes you've guessed it got THE Receptionist again and she told me the appointment would not be for another 4 days. I did point out the letter said urgent but she wouldn't budge on the date. Luckily enough for me, Viv the Clinician I had been dealing with had given me her e-mail address so I contacted her to explain what had happened and that I was also still having wee-wee problems. She called me back and we were both summoned to the Surgery to see her and the Doctor as the case was very complicated!! Now given the Covid situation and most consults were being done on the Phone, double panic set in. She tried to re-assure me not to panic and that they felt it would be easier to talk face to face. I wasn't convinced, and neither was Tim. We arrived at the Surgery to be greeted by Viv and the Doctor. We must have looked like Rabbits caught in headlights, but they done their best to re-assure us that they really just wanted to chat to us face to face. Anyway, the long and short of it was they were concerned about my iron levels, and they thought I could be Anaemic. Why they couldn't have done that on the phone I will never know, but we were grateful for them seeing us as it's easier to ask questions face to face. A blood test was arranged and the Doctor prescribed long term Anti-Biotics for the peeing problem. I had to take them one hour before bed. That night I had the best night's sleep I had experienced in ages!!! Could these tablets be the magic cure? I could only hope. The Bloods all came back fine, so panic over. My sugar levels were now stable, and the cough was getting better, and I was feeling a little more energetic. All seemed to be going in the right direction at last!!!!

TREATMENT THREE.

So, third round of treatment coming up. It still took 4 hours, but again that's a small price to pay for something you hope is going to help you get better. I had noticed the last couple of nights I had slept really well, and didn't seem to be weeing so much. I was still hoping the magic night time tablets were the answer to my prayers!!!!

Two days after the treatment I went into complete wipe out mode. I had expected this as it had happened after the first two rounds of treatment, but it was still a pain. I knew that it was going to last a few days, so decided just to give in and rest and sleep. Sometimes your body just tells you what to do, and to be honest the best thing you can do is listen to it. Fighting it can just make things worse.

A couple of days later the pee stinging was back. Now I was starting to be convinced it was the treatment, but I was now not so sure about the medication. As I have stated before with the stinging, when it was at its worst, it would hurt like hell and last for about one and a half hours. I had to put a cold compress on my noo-noo and take pain killers, which helped, but didn't alleviate the pain. When the pain eventually wore off it was such a relief. So, back to square one on the noo-noo problem! I contacted the Doctors again, and was told to up the night time medication to twice a day for 3 days and then go back to just taking it at night. I was starting to feel like I was banging my head against a brick wall and that I was going to be stuck with this problem forever! I just wished someone could have helped a little more as it was becoming quite apparent that what was being done was not working, but not being medically minded, I rightly or wrongly assumed they knew what they were doing.

In the meantime, Sharon the Cancer Nurse had called me and said that now it could be the Immunotherapy that was causing the stinging, which was a little strange as they thought it was the Chemo? So we now have, could be Chemo, Immuno, Diabetes, Cystitis, medication, or a whole host of other things. All I knew was that it was not getting any better and nothing seemed to be working. It's bad enough having to deal with the Cancer and the effects of treatment. The Peeing problem seemed to be dragging me down further. If only I could just get a good night's sleep.

I had an Appointment come through from the Hospital as they had arranged a CT scan with contrast, the one that makes you feel like you've wet yourself, for the 19th November. I was particularly worried about having this one done as I was weeing so much, and the thought that I might actually wet myself was very disturbing. On my last scan they said that no-one had actually done it and I really didn't relish the thought of being the first. You have to drink a fair amount of water before the scan and that was concerning me as well. I did call the unit to explain the situation and they didn't seem overly bothered but I sure as hell was. The idea of the scan is to check the size of the Tumour to see if the treatment is working, and to also see of the Cancer had spread elsewhere. The Oncologist was due to phone me at the beginning of December, two weeks after the Scan. That was going to be a long 2 weeks.

I took a call from an actual Doctor from the surgery as she wanted to discuss Blood results, which was a bit odd as I hadn't had any more done! We had a long discussion about my Urinary problem, and yes you've guessed it, she was at a loss as to what was causing it. She wanted to try another course of Anti-Biotics which I agreed to and she also requested another Urine sample. I sometimes wondered about the amount of Anti-Biotics I was being prescribed and to be quite frank with you they really were not making that much difference, but as I said before, I'm not medically minded so just kept on taking them.

The Doctor did say that she didn't think it was the medication I was on that was causing the problem, and it was nothing I was doing that was making it worse. I explained that the stinging seemed to be more inside the

Urethra and she stated that it could possibly be inflamed. That made a lot of sense to me. Although the stinging would be there sometimes when I Weed, sometimes when I finished, or just randomly sting when I was sitting down, inflammation made a lot of sense to me. I felt like we may be getting somewhere. I did ask about taking Anti-Inflammatories but because of all the different medication I was on that was not possible. Back to square one. I done the Urine sample and Viv the Clinician called to say it was all clear and that the Doctor would call me the next day. She never called.

My days now were just mulling into one. Good day, bad day, tired day, more awake day! Stinging nearly every day and not much sleep! On good days I could manage a little exercise which made me feel a little better but I wanted to do more. (Once an Athlete, always an Athlete).

I am going to go off track a little here. Now we all hear horror stories about treatments for Cancer, and when they say it's brutal, there is no escaping from the fact that it is. There are various different treatments available for different types of Cancer from Surgery, Chemotherapy, Immunotherapy, and Radiotherapy and probably a lot more that I don't know about. Everyone seems to respond differently depending on the type of treatment they receive. Now at this point and you're going to think me a little strange, as I felt very lucky and grateful for the side effects I was having with my treatment. I was just more wiped out and tired, slightly sore and dry mouth and occasionally felt a little sick, but the magic pills they gave me soon sorted that out. Constipation was a bit of a problem, but a wonder liquid called Lactulose sorted that out, but boy did it give me wind. I was advised to try other liquids but I found this one worked for me, so I was stuck with it farts and all!!!! I was very lucky in the fact that my hair didn't fall out, much to Tim's disappointment as the clippers finally went to bed. Joking apart, it was nice to know he would have been there in my hour of need. Not many people would have been comfortable with that but he was. Speaking to other Cancer patients and hearing some of their horror stories, and I don't think it fair to go into any details as its very personal to each person, hopefully you can now understand why I felt lucky and grateful.

TREATMENT FOUR.
EUREKA MOMENT!!!!

The pre-assessment went well for the next round of treatment, and there were no problems with the Bloods. The day before every treatment I had to start on a course of Steroids 4mg in the morning and 4mg at lunchtime, which is quite a high dose! I had to do this for 3 days. And this is where the Eureka moment kicked in!!!! I suddenly realised that when I had been taking the Steroids before my treatments the stinging was less and I was sleeping better. The times I was on the medication I hadn't really notice it as I was being pumped with all sorts to try and sort out the Peeing problem. But on this occasion it was noticeable. On doing some re-search, I discovered that Steroids are Anti-Inflammatories!!! BOOM!!!!! Could this be the answer to my prayers?? As I had a suspected inflamed Urethra it seemed a bit obvious to me. I called Sharon to explain, and after she had been in touch with the Oncologist, who was a little concerned it may interfere with some of the treatment, she agreed that it was worth a try. Fingers crossed!

The 4th treatment went well and took the compulsory four and a half hours, but at least I got lunch this time and went prepared with things to do. The team in the Cancer unit were amazing as usual.

This was to be the last round of treatment with the brutal regime of double Chemo and Immunotherapy. I was also under the impression it was the last of the Chemo and that I would just be on Immunotherapy after this treatment. Again I could not have been more wrong. I was given an appointment card for my next round of treatment, and it was for one lot of Chemo and Immunotherapy, and there would be four rounds of this. I was gutted. I think this may have been mentioned at the initial consult with the Oncologist, but there was just so much to take in I seemed to have overlooked that statement. The good news on this was that the toxic Chemo, the one that makes you feel rough was being dropped so the hope was that the treatment would not be quite so brutal and the side effects more manageable. This did knock me back a bit, but I realised everyone was doing this for my own welfare, so once I spoke to Tim and got my head around it I was cool with it. What did make me feel a lot brighter was the fact I was starting to sleep better, the stinging of the Urethra was not so bad and I was not using the potty so much at night. I strongly started to believe that the Steroids were in part a solution to the problem. Don't get me wrong, the problem was still there, but a lot better.

The day after my treatment I was booked in for a basic Scan of the lower Abdomen to see if they could spot anything going on that would explain the Urinary problem which had been arranged by Amanda at the Doctors. Again I had concerns as I had to have a full bladder and that was going to prove almost impossible as I was weeing so much, especially when I drank something.

I did explain this to them and they were fine about it and said not to worry. After the Ultrasound they explained that there was nothing at all to get anxious about except for a very small Cyst on the Kidney. I'm not really sure if they were supposed to tell me or not but I was very grateful that they did, as they were very re-assuring as to there being nothing to be concerned about. They were sending the report through to the Doctors and I was to receive a call from them in a few days.

I had all of the usual post treatment side effects, but they somehow seemed a little more manageable this time round. I was still falling asleep a lot, but I was also sleeping better at night. They say you can slay Dragons after a good night's sleep!!! In my case maybe just little ones! After about 5 days of wipe out I really started to feel much, much better and actually managed to stay awake for a whole day, which again in turn helped me sleep at night. I was starting to feel good and very positive about things.

About eight days after my treatment, on the 19th November, I had the CT Ultrasound which was the one that would be sent to the Oncologist to determine whether the treatment was working or not. I felt very proud of myself with this one as I actually managed to walk to the Hospital!! Something I had not been able to do for ages, and it was so nice to be outside and get some fresh air. This was going to be an anxious wait, but hopefully one worth waiting for. It was going to be a long two weeks.

Things were really starting to look up for me, and I was feeling the best I had felt in months. My breathing was better, the cough seemed a lot less than it was before and the Peeing problem was continuing to be less of an issue, and I was managing to stay awake during the day. I could now manage seven and a half minutes on the Treadmill and Bike, and I could actually start to feel my muscles in my legs beginning to form again. This gave me so much hope and made me feel good about myself. Housework was once again a joy!!

By now we were into November, and I was starting to think about Christmas. We were in another lock-down, so it was going to be just me and Tim at home together to celebrate the festive season. We were both absolutely fine with this as we were more than comfortable in each other's company. I did have a lot of concerns though. After being told by Dr Cominos that I may only have three months to a year, and bearing in mind all of the mishaps and problems I had encountered, I was concerned, rightly or wrongly, that I might not make Christmas. A very morbid thought, but I'm sure you will agree one that had to be taken into account. Me being me though, I still went Gung-Ho into arranging Christmas. It was my job to organise all of the food and presents, a job that over the years I have enjoyed so much, and Tim takes over on Christmas day and does all of the cooking and making the day very special. I must admit, given the circumstances I did go a little over the top, well actually a lot, but it kept me busy and took my mind of things.

Because we couldn't go to the shops as I had to shield due to my Immune system being compromised, our front door was permanently busy with deliveries of food and gifts. It just made me feel excited every time we had a delivery!!! I was constantly on the lap top sorting thing out, but this made me very happy as although I was still tired and not as mobile as I would have liked to have been, my brain was still in top gear!! The cupboards and Freezers were getting full of food and Presents were arriving in abundance!!

Up until now I had managed to get my Treadmill and Bike regime up to seven and a half minutes, but now I found myself managing ten on both. I was not so sleepy and was coping with things I couldn't before. Life was looking good.

I was due for my next round of treatment at the beginning of December, but then I realised that the one after that was going to fall 3 days before Christmas. Now given I had concerns about Christmas, understandably, I wanted to at least try and make it special if I could. I did ask Sharon if it could be postponed for a week or two, but if it was going to be to the detriment of my health and welfare I didn't have a problem having it done. She got back to me after she had spoken to Dr Cominos and said it had been postponed to the begging of January. Christmas and New Year were starting to look a lot brighter.

One of the things that you learn you have to do when going through treatment and the effects that come with it is to become the master of the Curve Ball. Tim's Birthday was going to fall on the same week as my treatment, which was very sad as I wanted to make it special for him, and I suspected that I may be too tired for it to be the Birthday he deserved. However, in a moment of genius I decided to bring it forward a week!! It would mean we could celebrate his big day with me feeling good, as I knew that I would, and if I felt good on treatment week then we could celebrate twice!!! His Birthday was perfect.

The next round of treatment only took two and a half hours which was a bonus and it went well. Sharon the Cancer Nurse came to see me before my treatment and I was telling her about how well I was feeling and she agreed that I was looking really good.

The only concern I had was that in 2 days' time we had the Consultation with Dr Cominos and that I was very worried about the results. She said that the Scan results should reflect the way I felt, and as I was feeling good it made me feel a little more positive, and she also explained that everyone felt the same, and it was commonly known as 'Scanxiety'. That sort of made sense! The day before receiving the results I was feeling very apprehensive and didn't sleep to well but due to what Sharon had said, and the fact I felt so well, we were hoping for positive results.

THE RESULTS ARE IN.

December 3rd 2020. The day of judgement had arrived. I don't think either of us slept that well but it was hardly surprising. Due to the Covid crisis, we could not attend the Hospital for a face to face Consultation, and the telephone call was due to come to us at 10am. At least we didn't have to wait until the afternoon. That would have been unbearable. It's surprising just how slow time can go when your waiting for something as important as a call like this, and I can never get my head around how quick time goes when you are enjoying yourself, and I can assure you we were not. We talked a lot about different outcomes, bracing ourselves for the worst, hoping for the best. 10am came and went. Then 10.15am and 10.30am, and 10.45am, talk about prolonging the agony. I fully understand that the medical professionals were very busy at that moment in time, but this was agony. So here we go.

10.55am the call finally came in.

Dr Cominos didn't waste any time and went straight to the results. The Tumour had shrunk significantly and the Cancer had not spread anywhere else. Yes you read that right, shrunk and not spread. She was very, very happy with the results and needless to say, so was Tim and myself. She said we would continue with the treatment plan; re-scan in 6 weeks and to arrange another consultation in 3 months. At this point I completely broke down. I just couldn't stop crying. The news we had just received was better than winning the Lottery, and from the bottom of my heart I really do mean that. It was possibly going to take a few days to sink in but we were both just so happy, we could cope with that. She didn't actually have any measurements or percentage of shrinkage, but significantly is a big word and to me meant it had shrunk a lot. She also said that my breathing should be a bit better and she was right. It was. She was still at a loss as to what was causing the Urinary problem and she was possibly thinking of stopping the Chemo, but with results like that I was not too keen on that idea and wanted to carry on as the side effects were no-where near as bad as before. They were not great but bearable. I still couldn't stop crying. They were happy tears. We couldn't thank her enough, and that was that, the call ended.

I think we were both a little stunned. There should have been more questions, and we even had a list but that all went out of the window with news like that. We hugged, laughed and made rather loud 'whoop-whoop' noises and couldn't stop smiling and giggling, and yes, I had stopped crying by now.

After we had calmed down, we let the family know the good news. Needless to say there were more tears and I think they were all so relieved and happy for us. And then we let every swinging dick know!! A lot of our friends and work colleagues had kept in touch throughout this Journey so I felt it only right to let them all know the good news. There were rather a lot of them but it was such a pleasure to share this with them and I didn't care how long it was going to take. Needless to say they were all over the Moon as well. Sharon had been right. The results had reflected the way I was feeling. I just needed to stay focused on feeling good for the foreseeable future to continue to at least put up the best fight I possibly could against the Cancer. I cannot describe going from the worst day ever in July, to probably one of the best days ever in December. What a journey so far. Thank you, Thank you, and Thank you.

In the meantime, we took a call from the Doctor's surgery from one of the Clinicians, not one of my special ones but a different one, to say that they wanted to arrange a CT scan on the Kidney and Renal area to see if there was anything there that was causing the Peeing problem. I agreed and they were going to arrange it. Also, I don't know if you remember but my Lung had partially collapsed? I had been taking a puffer every day for this as when they told me about the collapsed lung it had caused COPD. (Chronic Obstructive Pulmonary Disease) the name for a group of Lung conditions that causes breathing difficulties. The Doctors had also received the report from the Oncologist and informed me of the good news that the Lung had started to inflate itself. I didn't know it could do that but it was. So with the good news we had from the Oncologist, the Doctors on the ball with the Urinary problem and the Lung sorting itself out, the day was looking very sunny and rosy. Oh, and I managed 15 minutes on the Treadmill and Bike!!!

I now had 6 weeks treatment free and it was going to be interesting to see how I felt. I was comfortable with the time off as I knew Dr Cominos wouldn't do that unless it was safe for me. I was still a little sceptical about Christmas, but the way I was starting to feel filled me with a lot of hope. The days just seemed to be getting better and better, and I was having odd moments of feeling semi-normal, whatever that was these days. I was still managing my exercises, and doing housework, and managing to order everything online as we were in lock-down again and I was still shielding. I must admit I was quite happy to just stay at home because the idea of catching Covid was a very scary thought with my condition. Basically if I caught it the chances were I would not survive it. That did present a few problems as I was paranoid about touching anything that had been delivered. However, good hand washing and Sanitiser were the order of the day. Tim did have to go out on a few occasions and I would batter him with staying safe and away from people, wearing a mask and sanitising his hands. He really didn't need me to tell him any of this but it made me feel better. I knew he would never do anything to put me at risk.

I had been advised to try and come off the Steroids by Dr Cominos, so I decided to give it a try. I was on 2mg a day, so I was to reduce that to 2mg every other day and then stop. I was a bit sceptical, but I really didn't want to be on them as they can cause side effects, and although they seemed to be working for the Urinary problem, it would be interesting to see if it was them that were helping. The problem with coming off the Steroids is that it can make you a little more tired until the body adjusts which can take up to a week. Didn't mind that too much, but a week after coming of the Steroids the stinging was back. So now we knew for sure that they were working to alleviate the problem. I phoned Sharon to explain what had happened, and Dr Cominos reluctantly agreed for me to go back on them.

I did ask Sharon if there was an alternative Anti-Inflammatory I could use, and she didn't know so advised me to call the Doctors for advice. I spoke to one of the Clinicians, not one of my special ones I must add, and she didn't know of any either so advised me to stay on the Steroids until the referral came through. I did ask her what was happening with the Referral, but she said once it had been sent it was out of their hands, and it was up to me to chase it up myself. I really didn't find that very helpful at all and actually thought it was a bit of a cheek.

It had been 3 weeks since the Referral was done, so I was surprised I had not heard anything. I tried to chase it up, and left messages for people to call me back, but no-one did and again I felt like I was getting no-where fast. It was just so frustrating again that no one would help me. I decided to call Viv, one of my lovely Clinicians to see if she could help. I explained everything to her, and she e-mailed the Urology department to see what was happening. Apparently, my appointment was for the 1st February but they were going to try and bring it forward. Some things you just cannot sort out yourself! Thank God for Viv. The appointment came through within a few days for the 17th January. So back on the Steroids at least until such a time that the peeing problem was sorted! At least I tried.

CHRISTMAS.

As I have said before, it had been a family tradition for a few years that on Christmas day, we would all be on the phone together at 11am to raise a toast to dearly departed family and friends. My Dad was now living away from us with his lady friend Audrey who I must say was an absolute treasure, and really good for him and we were more than happy with their situation. We had spent many Christmas's together over the last few years, always having an amazing time. This year, because of circumstances and Covid that sadly could not happen! However, with all the new Technology, we decided it would be a good idea to do a Zoom call on Christmas day. Now bear in mind, Dad was 83 and not too Techno savvy, we decided to do a dummy run before Christmas. And that is exactly what it was!!!!! It took ages just to set it all up. We were in, we were out, we could see them then we couldn't, we could hear them then we couldn't. Boy it was hard work, but with patience and two hours of our lives we were never going to get back we cracked it. I must admit once we had it all sorted it was just so great to actually see them on the screen. Why we hadn't done it sooner I will never know. We then decided to have a dummy run with the rest of the family all together, and it was great. We were all set for Christmas day.

Only a few more days till Christmas and at last I was starting to get really excited. I was excited before, with a little trepidation, but now I was beginning to get ecstatic! All of the food was in, there were presents everywhere, and the house looked like a Fairy Grotto. I had managed to send cards and gifts to the rest of the Family, and they had sent ours to us as well. We just had so many gifts! I think myself and Tim did go over the top a bit with presents, well quite a lot actually, but why not. Why not indeed!

We had taken a few little drives out, mainly to collect Medication from the Pharmacy, but on one occasion we decided to drive a little further as we were out anyway, and I couldn't believe some of the Christmas lights we saw in gardens and on Houses. They were just so magical and there were just so many of them. People had really embraced the outside lights this year that's for sure. There were some that were just pure class, some that were just normal and some that were weird and wacky!!! Needless to say we done these drives a few times as boy did they put a smile on our faces!! Don't envy their bills in January though.

Before we knew it Christmas Eve had arrived. Another tradition we observe on Christmas Eve is to have hot Porky rolls at teatime. The meat is slow cooked during the afternoon, which in itself causes a problem. You would just not believe the smell that comes from the kitchen. It leaves you salivating all afternoon and the expectation of deliciousness is stunning. Tim was busy all afternoon preparing the feast for tomorrow and cooking the Pork. All my hard work was now done. It was over to the Boss!!!! Teatime came and we partook in a little drinkie and then absolutely devoured the porky rolls.

I think I may have had 3 but they were just so delicious, and to be honest I probably could have done 4!!!

We played games, which I won (all of them) and then settled down and watched a film. An amazing relaxing fun evening! Just what the Doctor ordered.

The big day arrived, and I can honestly say it could not have been more perfect. I had been worried something may go wrong with me and I was going to spoil the day, but I didn't need to worry. I felt great. It was Christmas day. I have to admit one of the first things I said to Tim in the morning was "I made it". He did seem a little surprised at this, but once I explained he fully understood. He also admitted that given all of the things I had been through earlier in the year, he was concerned as well, but as I had been feeling so good lately, he had stopped worrying and was confident all would be fine. Breakfast eaten, showers taken, and Tim finishing of his preparations, it was present time, and boy there did seem a lot. We had a lot of special gifts from friends and family, and I did seem to receive rather a lot of Penguin gifts. I do so love Penguins. The gifts that we bought for each other were astonishing, and considering it was hard to know what to give each other this year we did a great job. I won't bore you with the details, but just want to say I was blown away with all of my treasured gifts. The Zoom call came at 11am, and as we partook in Sherry and mince pies, raising our glasses to loved ones not present, it was obvious that this was a good idea and everyone was really enjoying it.

It was just so lovely to actually see everyone on Christmas day. It went exceptionally well and took about an hour, although I did have a hunch that Dad might have had a little too much of the Sherry bless him.

Tim was now full on in the kitchen and once again the smells were sublime. The anticipation of what was to come was overwhelming and I just couldn't wait.

2pm, Table set, Candles aglow, music on, it was time to feast. I have to admit that in the past I did like a drink before dinner, and probably over done it a little on several occasions, and although I would eat well, I didn't really eat that much, but enjoyed what I had. This year due to the Cancer I was sceptical about how much I could have to drink so only had a little. OMG what a difference! I just could not stop eating. This was the feast to beat all feasts. It was just so delicious. I did apologise to Tim for all the years I hadn't eaten so much but I more than made up for it this year. It was the soberest Christmas dinner ever for me but it made me appreciate and enjoy the food more. We had a little break now and played some table games for a while, until it went dark, then the Christmas pudding got it. It was presented at the table, it then had Brandy poured over it and set alight. Absolutely spectacular and delicious especially served with extra thick cream. The time was now 5.30pm. We do like to take our time. I am going to leave it there as I am now getting hungry, and I hope I haven't bestowed the same on you.

We settled down for the evening, relaxed and watched a couple of films, and that was that. Christmas done! I cannot even begin to tell you how grateful I was for the day, and how perfect it was.

With all the hard times we had both been through this year I think we both deserved the pleasure of the day.

The next few days were also really good days. I was feeling undeniably well and managing to walk outside and was still doing 15 minutes on the Treadmill and Bike. I was going to need that after what I ate!!! I didn't feel overly tired, Blood Sugars were good, and although the Peeing problem hadn't gone away completely, it was manageable. I had also managed to put my weight back on, and some!!!! All was good with life.

New year's eve arrived and we made another Zoom call with the family, which was great, and then, yes you've guessed it, Tim cooked a spectacular 4 course Dinner, which again took nearly 3 hours to complete eating. We again settled down, relaxed and watched films, but I must admit we didn't make the Bells. I was far too full and tired for that. Christmas and New Year had been a roaring success, and despite both of us having misgivings on the state of my health, it could not have been more perfect given the situation. It might be the last one I see, hopefully not, no one knows, but we both had one hell of a time.

Chapter 6

Coping.

LOCKDOWN AGAIN!!!!!

Happy New Year, and welcome to 2021. We were still reeling from the success of Christmas, and both agreed that we were both blessed and grateful to have had such an amazing time. It was perfect. It was now time to take the Decorations down, which made me a little sad as they looked so cheerful and bright. We didn't remove them from our Conservatory, which doubles as our dining room, as it was my Birthday at the end of January and I wanted them left up. Will let you know why later on!!!

The 5th of January saw us in yet another full lock-down. Things had got really bad with Covid again, and the amount of new cases and people dying was higher than it was in the first peak. The Government in their ultimate wisdom had relaxed the Covid restrictions over the Christmas period, allowing at least some families to be together over the Festive period. Some people thought it was a good idea, others didn't. Either way things were getting out of control, the NHS was again under enormous pressure. It was a very scary time. Although this was the third lock-down, it did seem like people were not really taking it that serious this time round. The roads seemed busier, and on the news people were still out and about, breaking all of the rules. I had been advised to shield again as I could not afford to catch the virus in my condition. This also meant that Tim was advised to shield as well to protect me. He really didn't mind at all as he was still working from home, and to be honest the weather was that bad we really didn't want to go out anyway. The only thing was I was getting really paranoid about the situation. Every time the Post or any Parcels came I made Tim open them and then wash his hands.

We had a situation without heating which meant someone had to come and fix it and that really freaked me out. I didn't want anyone else in our House but sadly I had no control over that as the heating needed to be fixed. Although the guy that came was really good and seemed safe enough it didn't stop me getting stressed.

I had to speak Sharon the Cancer Nurse as I was due for my next round of treatment on the 12th January and was concerned it may not go ahead. The NHS was overwhelmed with cases of Covid, and this meant that some of the other treatments were going by the wayside. She assured me everything would be fine and she was right.

I had my pre-treatment assessment on the 8th January, and there were no issues. I did mention that I had a really dry mouth and tingly hands and feet after the last treatment but was told that this was just down to the Chemo. The only thing was I had put on just over 4 kg in weight over Christmas, but I was not surprised and they didn't seem overly worried about it but I wasn't happy. That was a little much even by my standards. I had three more treatments to go for this round and then I wasn't sure if there would be any more Chemotherapy after that. I guess that would be down to Dr Cominos. I thought I would ask the Nurse if she knew. And I'm afraid that was not a good move on my part.

Imagine my shock and horror when she said I would be on Chemotherapy for two years. The thought of that filled me with dread. Now I know the Chemo is doing me the world of good, and was very grateful for that, but knowing how it makes one feel and having that every three weeks for two years was earth shattering. The problem being that a few days after the Chemo I would experience post treatment fatigue. I knew it was coming as it had every time, but it didn't mean I had to like it. The worst of the fatigue would last for about 3-4 days where all I could do was sleep, and then very slowly start to feel better. It made me feel very weak sometimes, and simple things became a lot harder to do. Very slowly over the week that followed, I found I could start to do little things again, a slow process, and about a week before the next treatment was due I would be back to feeling good again. So it's a very up and down process and maybe now you can understand more why two years of this was not giving me a feel good factor. I knew that I would have to stay on Immunotherapy for two years, as stated by the Oncologist, but I was not prepared for the Chemo. However, if it was to be then I would embrace it as I had with all of my treatment.

The 6th treatment was administered on the 12th January and all went well as usual. Again the Nurses were so busy but very efficient at what they done. They really are Angels.

I was still managing 15 minutes on the Treadmill and Bike, and was now starting to walk up and down the path in the garden to get some fresh air. I wouldn't go any further than that through fear of Covid. I was also managing a resistance band to help strengthen my arms and legs, and I am happy to say that my muscles were starting to come back, albeit very slowly, but they were there!!!! I was starting to feel good apart from post treatment fatigue setting in and the ongoing Urinary problem.

Sadly, the wee-wee problem was still there, but was not as bad as it had been and was manageable. I was still up three times a night but that was nothing compared to eight or nine times. I spoke to Sharon and explained that I wanted to stay on the Steroids until I had at least seen the Urologist, as they seemed to be working at keeping the stinging at bay. I had tried to stop them but the problem recurred so I just wanted to leave things as they were. I also asked her if she knew how long I was to be on Chemo for and she didn't know but confirmed the Immunotherapy was for two years. She also couldn't find out about the size of the shrinkage of the Tumour, which was a bit sad as we really would have liked to know. It seemed like no-one knew, but at least we knew it was significant.

There seemed to be some confusion over the CT scan that was booked for the 17th January. I thought it was for the Urologist but it turned out it was for the Oncologist. I was very troubled by this as Dr Cominos had said to repeat the scan in three months and only two had gone by. We were both concerned that this may not show a true reflection of the state of the Tumour. I explained everything to the Radiologist at the appointment and he confirmed it was Oncology that had requested the appointment be bought forward. I think what had happened was that when the Clinician had asked for the appointment to be bought forward for the Urologist, there had been a mix up and the request had actually gone to Oncology instead of Urology. So still nothing was happening about the peeing problem.

I sometimes don't know if I need an Oncologist, Urologist, Gynaecologist or a Psychologist!!! It just gets oh so confusing, as you can probably see.

For the last month or so, the Government had started to roll out the Covid vaccination programme. This was going to be a game changer in a lot of ways. They had split it into different categories, and the plan was to Vaccinate groups 1-4 by mid-February, that being the very elderly, care homes and clinically vulnerable people, a total of approximately 15 million individuals, with the rest of the population following in age groups descending. There had again been some uncertainty as to what group I fell into, as when I spoke to Amanda the Clinician at the Doctors a while ago she said I was in group 6, but I explained that I was now classed as extremely clinically vulnerable, and I thought I should be in group 4. She did say there was some confusion about this particular group and she would look into it for me. Sharon the Cancer Nurse also re-iterated that the group was confusing but she seemed to think I should be in group 4. The problem I was going to face was there was only a small window of opportunity for me to have the Vaccination. After Chemo, the body's Immune system becomes very vulnerable, and at around day 6-10 it is at its lowest. This soon picks up again, so by day 17-18, usually around the time of the pre-assessment the Immune system is as good as it is going to get. This gave me a window of approximately 4 days to get the vaccine done, as that was the amount of time there was between the assessment and treatment. I couldn't have it done until I had undergone my pre-assessments as the Bloods needed to be checked to make sure they were alright so I could have the jab.

This is where Viv the special Clinician exceeded everything I had asked of her.

I called her and explained the situation, and said that if I couldn't get it done on my next pre-assessment, I would have to wait another 3 weeks. Not that this would have been a problem, but it would have been nice to know I could get it done. I took a call from the Doctors to say my jab had been booked for Friday 29th January, the same day as my pre-assessment. Talk about timing!!! As long as my Bloods were alright I was good to go. Also, I was a little bit cheeky and asked about Tim's Vaccination. As he was now classed as my main carer, it had been said that carers were to come into the first phase of Vaccinations as well. Viv totally agreed, and he had his done the week before me. He did experience some side effects, mainly feeling Flu like and cold and shivery which worried me. However, after a hot bath, Paracetamol and a rather large Whisky he was fine after 24 hours much to my relief.

My bloods all came back fine after my pre-assessment and I was given the green light to go ahead with the Vaccination. I was a little apprehensive and anxious as I had seen on the Television queues of people at other Vaccination centres, not that I was adverse to queues, but I didn't relish the idea of getting quite that close to other people given the situation with Covid.

It had been arranged in a small Village Hall about 4 miles from our House. I really needn't have worried as the whole operation was a well-oiled machine. There were no queues of people, and it was just straight in, seated, a few questions asked, given the jab, waited 15 mins and then good to go. I really could not have felt safer. We were in and out in about 30 minutes, all done. I was lucky in as much as I didn't get the same side effects as Tim but my arm was sore for a few days. I had the Pfizer's jab and Tim had the Oxford one, and it had been said that the reaction from the Oxford vaccine was worse. Poor Tim! A sore arm was a small price to pay in my book, and as it was my Birthday tomorrow, I considered this to be one hell of a Birthday present. We were both just so grateful to have been given the opportunity to receive the Vaccine that we said we had both been injaculated!!! A joke that was to resonate with the rest of the family when they received theirs! Just a little pleasure joke on our part!

MY BIRTHDAY!!!!!!!

Saturday 30th January 2021. I made it!!! 60 today!!! What a milestone that was for me. Now a lot of people moan about getting older, and some even get a little out of sorts about hitting 60, but believe me when I say it was the most wonderful feeling to hit the big 6-0 and this is why I want to share it with you. Again I didn't know if I was going to make it or not, but here I was, 60 and proud. I have all my life seen Birthdays as special, and a privilege to be celebrated, and as Tim often says, getting older is unfortunately a privilege denied to so many. My Birthday was going to be magnificent, albeit hard work for poor Tim again.

Cast your mind back to when we took our Christmas decorations down. I mentioned that we had left the decorations up in our Conservatory which doubles as our dining room. This was because, wait for it, I wanted another Christmas day!!! And yes with all the trimmings, decorations music and all things Christmas!!! This was my wish for my Birthday. Under normal circumstances we would have either gone away somewhere to celebrate or had a party, or basically done whatever we wanted, but given my health condition and the fact we were in lock-down, it was going to be the two of us, at home on our own doing what we do best. Celebrating!

There were again presents everywhere from friends and family and of course Tim. I had been looking at these for days and was getting very excited. What was also good was that this was the weekend where I would feel my best before the next treatment. Talk about timing again. Tim had spent 2 days in the Conservatory doing 'things' and I wasn't allowed to go in there until it was time for dinner, and no I wasn't tempted to peek. Well maybe I was just a little but I didn't.

I woke up in the morning very excited as you would expect, and we done the same as we had done at Christmas. Breakfast, showers and the unveiling of the gifts! I again won't bore you with all of the details of my presents, but the best gift I got was a Piano Keyboard (as well as a new Laptop). I used to play Keyboard years ago when we were Entertainers, but had never mastered the art of reading the little dots on a sheet of music. I had decided a little while ago that it was something I would love to learn, and lo and behold a Piano Keyboard was within in my grasp. This was going to be a long process but one I was determined to master.

We done another zoom call with the family at 11am which was so enjoyable as again it was so lovely to see them, and it was so nice to celebrate a part of my day with the people who are most precious to me. This bought a little tear to my eyes, in a good way.

4.30pm and it was time for pre-dinner Sherry, and then at 5pm Tim called me through to the dining room.

OMG I could not believe what I saw. Not only did we have the Christmas decorations up, but there were Balloons, Banners, extra lights and dangly things everywhere, not to mention a perfectly laid table with candles and wine. It just all looked so perfect. We had Pork instead of Turkey, but apart from that everything was the same as Christmas and just as delicious and yes I ate just as much. The feast was washed down with a beautiful bottle of Chateau-Neuf-De-Pape, a little luxurious but one I think was befitting of such a special day given the circumstances. Tim had also bought a table Quiz game with the questions all relating to the number 60!! Pure genius! As always dinner lasted for hours, and we snuggled down and watched a film. I can honestly again say I had the most perfect day, and even if we had managed to get away, or had gone out for dinner, I don't think I could have enjoyed it any more than I did, and with your kind permission I would like to say a huge thank you to Tim for making my day so special.

Oh boy, Sunday morning was not funny. I woke up and I must admit I felt a little rough. I had definitely overdone the food and wine and I think I had a bit of a hangover. Now over the years I had experienced a few of them, but since this journey had started I had not had any. I had forgotten how bad they can make you feel, and I sure as hell wasn't going to let that happen again. (Unless I make 65)! Having said that, it was my Birthday and in a strange way it was worth it. As the morning wore on I must admit I was feeling a lot better and by the afternoon was back to my usual self. Tim was suffering a little too and I did feel for him when I saw the washing up. We didn't have the luxury of a dish washer and the dirty plates, cutlery and glasses were everywhere but he managed to wade his way through it with his usual Military precision, and in no time at all it was done. We just relaxed for the rest of the day. A perfect weekend!

BACK TO NORMALITY.

I took a call from one of the Nurses from the Cancer unit on the Monday morning saying that my Cortisol Blood levels were very low following my pre-treatment Blood test last Friday, and this could make me feel more tired. I must admit, I didn't actually notice being more weary than normal, as I was in and out of sleepy spots most of the time.

She did say that I may need Steroids, which I was already taking, and that she was going to contact Dr Cominos as I was due for my next treatment tomorrow. She said she would call me back in the afternoon. Again she never called. The other worrying thing from my point of view was that the Nurse had called me last Friday to let me know that the Bloods were all fine and that it was alright for me to go and have the Covid vaccination, which I done. All was fine with the jab so no damage occurred, but it was still a little concerning.

We done the usual thing and went straight onto Google to find out more about raised Cortisol levels. Needless to say that again wasn't one of the best ideas as the main thing that can cause the levels to rise is stress, but there was also a lot of other things it could have been. If you want to worry yourself silly then this is the way to do it. There is a lot of information on-line but caution has to be the word of the day. Also you have to learn to ask more questions and be a pain in the 'butt'. I know I should have asked the Nurse for more information, but I didn't think quickly enough. However, I did manage to contact Sharon and explain to her what had been said, and she seemed to think it was the Steroids I was on that were causing the problem! That really was very confusing to me, as the Nurse had said I might need to go on Steroids? My money was on stress.

The Nurse had not called me back by 5.30, so I decided to call the Cancer unit myself to find out if my treatment was going ahead tomorrow or not. It's something I don't like to do as I know how busy they are and always seem short Staffed, but I really needed to know, so in this case I felt it was justified. I was given the thumbs up for tomorrow which was a bit of a relief, mainly because I didn't want another break in my treatment, and the Bloods couldn't have been that bad otherwise it wouldn't have gone ahead. All went well with the treatment on the Tuesday.

So it was all back to normal on the Monday, but I must admit I was still buzzing a little from my Birthday weekend. We had managed to structure our days, which was very important given the fact we were in lock-down, and we were both shielding, so we couldn't get out. I was filling up my days with housework, playing the Piano, which by the way was going very well albeit a little slow and plonky, and writing this book. On-line shopping was great. We were ordering quite a lot of nice things for the House and for personal use, and we were almost on first name terms with the delivery driver!!! Food shopping was fun as well. I was managing to secure a home delivery shop every week, which was just as well because we would not have actually been able to go to the Supermarket. The anticipation of all the goodies coming on a Wednesday was enjoyable. Would it arrive on time? Would it all be there? Would it all fit in the Fridge and Freezer? Questions that arose every week, but apart from a few substitutions the anticipation was met without a hitch.

Obviously at the moment I couldn't go back to work, and the blessing was that Tim was working from home due to the Covid situation. If he had not been I feel we may have had a huge problem on our hands given my situation, but it was all working out perfectly.

He had decided to take an online course in Positive Psychology, something he had been interested in for years, and boy did he smash it!!!! He managed 100% in all of his course work, and passed with a Distinction. I was so proud of him, and I think he was very proud of himself. Not to let an opportunity pass him by, he took another course on-line for Mindfulness, and achieved the same outstanding results!!! The lovely thing was that the company he worked for asked him to put some courses together to be delivered on-line to all their staff. He was chuffed as punch at being asked to do this, and consequently delivered the most amazing courses, which judging by the feedback from the participants, had gone down exceptionally well!!!

I was starting to feel a little better every day, still managing my time on the Treadmill and Bike, my sugar levels were now mostly normal, I was sometimes tired and sometimes not, the cough had gone completely, and life was starting to feel good. But yes, you've guessed it, the wee-wee problem was still there. This had now been going on since last September and to be honest I really was at my wits end to know what to do. It just seemed like no one was prepared to help. I called the Doctors again who advised me to call the Urology Department myself to chase it up again, but I couldn't get through to anyone and although I left messages, no-one got back to me. I decided to call Sharon to see if she could help as I felt I was banging my head against a brick wall. Luckily she had a friend who worked in Urology, so she spoke to her on my behalf, and it turned out the Doctors had sent a referral request on 2nd December 2020, and that Urology had e-mailed them back straight away to ask them to arrange a Renal CT scan with contrast. As we were now at Friday 5th February I realised that something had possibly gone wrong. I was not overly impressed, but decided not to get out of sorts until I had all the facts. I contacted Viv at the Doctors and she informed me that a request by e-mail had been sent to the Scan department on 3rd December. I called the department and they said they had never received it. All sounded a bit dodgy to me. Viv said she was going to send it again, so hopefully now things might start to move along.

A LITTLE WOBBLE.

Throughout this journey, I had tried my best to stay upbeat and positive. It hasn't always been easy given that just about everything that could have gone wrong probably has, and every now and then I had what I called a little wobble. Your brain can play so many tricks with you. You start to doubt everything like, I am ever going to feel better, how long have I really got? Is this as good as its going to get, especially after treatment when you are your lowest ebb? Then there is the guilt.

Relying on other people to look after you, feeling like you're letting people down, and feeling sad for the people around you even though you think it's you going through the worst of it. In essence it's not just you. Everyone around you, Family, Friends and especially those closest to you are going through exactly the same, but in different ways. I must admit myself and Tim have been very blessed in this department. We are open and honest with each other about our feelings and there are no Taboo subjects. This may not work for everyone, but it certainly did for us, but it didn't stop me feeling sorrowful for him.

I remember I woke up one morning and felt particularly grumpy. On this occasion, and I don't know for what reason, but I didn't talk to Tim about it. I wrote it all down on paper. I guessed if I wrote it down it would be out of my head and I would feel better. I was starting to feel fed up and frustrated at not being able to do as much as I wanted. I knew I was doing alright but wanted more. I was fed up with feeling tired and although my breathing was better it still wasn't right. I was still out of breath climbing the stairs. My hands and feet would often tingle, especially when I was tired, and it seemed that every-time I tried to mention any of the problems I was having to the Nurses on the unit at my pre-assessments, the reply would always be, oh it's the Chemo, which it probably was, but that didn't help me. Sharon didn't call as much as she used to, but she was under the impression I was doing really well, which I was, but I missed our calls. I was starting to feel a little abandoned medically. I knew I was coping effectively with the exercise, and my brain wanted to do more but the body said "No" and then you start to think is this as good as its going to get, a very horrid thought. We didn't have the appointment with the Oncologist for another 4 weeks, so I knew I would feel like this for at least that amount of time, and I still didn't know how long I was going to be on Chemo. The thought of 2 more years still ringing in my ears, and filling me with dread! I was trying everything I could to make myself feel better but sometimes I felt like I was getting nowhere.

The peeing problem was dragging me down as well, as it seemed to have been going on for so long and I was starting to think that no-one cared. I was still experiencing the stinging and up several times at night. Also I was sometimes very thirsty, and it seemed every time I drank something I would need to wee almost straight away. I still couldn't help thinking there had been a 'balls up' at the Doctors, and I felt they should have been more on the ball. I had tried to sort it out myself, a position I really didn't think I should have been put in. I also wanted to get off the Steroids, but they seemed to be the only thing that helped with the peeing problem. I really just wanted to feel well again. So there was my little wobble. It did help putting my thoughts onto paper, and as I said earlier the Brain can play some naughty tricks on you when you least expect it, and you are at your lowest. On this particular morning I had the Television on, and after writing my wobble on paper, I turned my attention to the TV. Talk about putting things into perspective. There was a young boy on the TV who had Leukaemia. He had gone through extensive treatment and had another 3 more years of treatment to go. He was taking everything in his stride, and seemed happy and positive. He was coping with it. It made me stop and realise just how lucky I was, and to stop feeling sorry for myself. I still got this!!!! I wish him well.

At this point I let Tim read what I had written down as I thought it was important to share my feelings with him. He pointed out to me that every February I seemed to suffer with something called SAD (seasonally adjusted disorder) and it had been going on for years, and do you know what, he was right, and that explained a lot. Talk about the voice of reason. It just goes to prove a point that it's not always best to bottle things up. Talking really is the best medicine. So wobble over, my day just got better and better.

GETTING PRO ACTIVE.

I decided, on the advice of Sharon, to try and cut the Steroids down to 1mg instead of 2mg a day to see if the stinging associated with the peeing problem came back, and sadly after 4 days it started again so back on 2mg daily.

At this point I really had had enough of this problem and decided to get more pro-active with it. I called the Surgery and wanted an appointment to actually talk to a Doctor. Now don't get me wrong here, my special Clinicians had been amazing, but I decided it was time to call in the Doc. I also called the Radiology department reference the CT scan. They had received the referral from the Doctors, but I was told it was only for a routine scan and they were not booking any at the moment. I think you can probably guess how I felt!!!

The Doctor called me in the afternoon, and couldn't apologise enough for the situation. I had written everything down, including dates when I had spoken to people and I gave him a complete run down of the whole situation. I did say it was bad enough having to deal with Cancer, and that this other problem had gone on for far too long and it was really dragging me down now. I pointed out to him I was still weeing 3-4 times a night and he was mortified I was having to climb the stairs that many times a night as our Bathroom was downstairs. I didn't have the heart to tell him about the Potty!!! He asked me to leave it with him and he would see what he could do. Again I really was not holding out much hope. He did agree I had been let down. In fairness to him, he did call me back, and said he had been onto the Radiology department and spoken to the on call Radiologist who agreed my case was urgent, and he would give the go ahead for the scan to be done. I was to call the department the next day and they would make an appointment for me. We were getting somewhere. I done as I was told and called them the next day only to be told they don't make appointments over the phone. They had received the urgent request, but it was going to take up to 4 weeks to get an appointment. I could have cried. The positive side of this was that at least I was in the system. I called the Doctors back, and basically I was just going to have to wait.

Strangely enough, Amanda called out of the blue so I explained everything to her and she was not happy. She said she was going to e-mail Radiology and see what she could do. True to her word, she came up trumps! She called me the next day to inform me that the CT scan was booked in on the Saturday, 2 days away!!!! Apparently, as they had said, it wasn't going to be done for at least another 4 weeks but the department agreed to bring it forward. She obviously worked her magic as she had done on many occasions throughout this Journey. She said she was also going to get in touch with Urology to chase that up, and see what she could do regarding our second Covid vaccines. Viv and Amanda, my two special Clinicians, really were there for me when I needed them and God only knows how I would have got through this without them. They were Superstars and I will be eternally grateful for everything they have done for me.

Friday 19th February saw my next pre-treatment assessment. I did tell the Nurse about some side effects I had encountered, being fatigue, tingly hands and feet, sore and dry mouth and constipation, but I was again told that these were down to the Chemo. She did look in my mouth and thought I had oral thrush, so I was to contact the Doctors for some medication. I contacted Viv and she sorted it straight away.

The CT scan was done on Saturday 20th February and went without a hitch, so it was just a case of waiting for the results. Now I know this may sound a little weird, but part of me wanted them to find something, as this would explain the peeing problem, but part of me wanted it to all be normal. Talk about a head mess. I just wanted this issue to go away.

I hope you don't mind but I'm going to digress a little here. My heart was going out during the Covid Pandemic to those people who had no one and were very lonely, people missing Family and Friends, and also some suffering Mental Health problems due to the Covid situations, and to all the people who had lost loved ones, Family or friends. But, a lot of people during lock-down were moaning and winging about what they couldn't do, like going to the Pub, having Haircuts, going to the Theatre or Football matches. Tim and I believe the whole Pandemic brings life into sharp perspective, and not only encourages people to re-evaluate things, but also, with the right mind-set can enable people to become a little more creative!

We used to love going to the Theatre and came up with a unique way of bringing it to us!!! We had pre-show drinks at home, followed by a pre-Theatre dinner (in our Conservatory). Tim moved the sofa directly in front of the Television, giving us front row seats, and we even dressed up in our finest clothes for the occasion. We settled down with excitement to watch the 25th anniversary show of Les Miserable with surround sound!!! It was just like being there!!! Just goes to prove what you can achieve when you think outside the box and put your mind to it. A perfect evening!

The next treatment took place on Tuesday 23rd February and all went well again, but I was so tired post treatment I was in bed by 9pm. The good thing was that I was starting to sleep a lot better now, and only weeing 2-3 times a night which really helped. Things always seem so much easier to cope with when you have a decent night's sleep!!!!

On the Thursday, Viv called with my scan results and they were all clear. In one way I must admit I was relieved, but it still didn't get to the root of the problem. Viv was going to again refer it to the Urologist for a Cystoscopy, where they place a Camera in the Urethra, and up into the Bladder to see what's going on. She also seemed to think I had something called Peripheral Neuropathy, the tingling in the hands and feet, which may have been affecting my Urethra. So now we had another 'could be' scenario to add to the list of what we had before!!! I was at a loss of where we were going with this next, but all I know is I wanted it sorted. Also on the Thursday I had my usual post-treatment fatigue set in and I knew it would last for another couple of days so this time I just gave in and relaxed with it.

Over the weekend we noticed that my blood sugar levels were on the high side and we were slightly concerned. So on the Monday we decided to call the Diabetic Nurse at the Doctors. We got 'The Receptionist' again and she really wasn't helpful as usual. She said she would speak to her to see if she needed to call me. In the past the Diabetic Nurse had said if I had any problems then I was to call her. I had a problem, I called, and she didn't call back. However, I did have the number for the Community Diabetic Nurse so I gave them a call as well. Within a very short space of time someone called me back. It transpired that I was eating too many Carbohydrates that were raising my sugar levels, and making me feel more tired and thirsty!!! I had started eating more bread and pasta as I thought they were healthy, but as usual I was wrong!!! So bread and pasta out, and my sugar levels returned to normal within a few days. Always learning on this journey!!!!

I had to have another Blood test at the Doctors for my Diabetes, Kidney function and Cholesterol and I was again having trouble getting the results. When I eventually spoke to a Receptionist (not THE one) it all got a little confusing as she said they needed to be repeated the Bloods but she didn't know why. I did ask to speak to someone who would know, but was told there was no-one available, and I couldn't get an appointment for 2 weeks, which worried me a little as now I would have to wait. However, Amanda called me the next day and the good news was that my Diabetic Bloods were at a good level but my Kidney and Cholesterol functions were a bit abnormal and that's why the bloods needed to be repeated next week. At least I now knew why they needed to be done again. Amanda did offer me Medication for the Cholesterol but I declined as I wanted to try and manage it myself, and I was already on enough pills and didn't really want anymore!!!

We were coping very well with the situation, with me continuing to manage more exercise, little by little my sleeps were getting so much better and I wasn't weeing so much at night. Also I found I wasn't so tired during the day. Tim continued to deliver his Positive Psychology courses at his work place and they were going really well. I had my Bloods repeated, and also had a Diabetic Eye test done as they like to make sure that there are no problems with the eyes caused by Diabetes. Thankfully the results came back about a week later and all was fine.

2nd ONCOLOGIST REVIEW.

We had an appointment on Thursday 11th March for another review with Dr Cominos the Oncologist. This time it was to be face to face and we went prepared with a list of questions. As before, we were both a little sceptical as you really don't know what's going to be said. Again we really needn't have worried. The Tumour was stable and had shrunk again and the Cancer had not spread anywhere else!!!! Music to our ears!!! The good news was that Dr Cominos said it was time to come off the Chemotherapy but I would remain on the Immunotherapy. She did also confirm that all of the side effects I had been feeling were down to the Chemotherapy, which was nice to hear from the head honcho!!! The collapsed Lung was still inflating, and she said I couldn't over exercise, but I just had to listen to my body. We did ask her about my Cancer being stage 4, as we had done some re-search and stage 4 normally means it has spread elsewhere. She explained that the Cancer was in the Lung lining as well so that was why it was classed as stage 4. At least it was all in one place and localised so that was good news. Dr Cominos was also convinced that it was the Chemo that was causing my Urinary problem. I was to have another scan in 6 weeks, and another review in 3 months.

Again we were over the moon with the results, and treated ourselves on the way home at our usual fast food outlet. We arrived home and shared our good news with all of the family, and as before we let every swinging dick know!!! We had some amazing messages come back to us, and we really appreciated the fact that everyone cared so much.

We have amazing neighbours in our area, and one of them brings me either Chocolate or Grapes and Magazines every week, and her kindness always touches my heart. Another one sometimes brings me Flowers, and on one occasion she asked Tim if she could put me on her prayer list at her Church. I was so touched by this that it actually made me cry. Such a beautiful kind thought, and it's so nice to know that there are still some genuinely kind people in this world.

Friday 12th March was my next pre-assessment day, and all went well apart from the fact that one of the Nurses noticed my face was very red. They also spotted that I had a rash on my arms, back and chest. I really hadn't noticed anything abnormal, and I wasn't itchy at all. They seemed again to think it was the Chemo and Steroids and they were going to e-mail Dr Cominos. Again they didn't get back to me. Also they informed me that I could now have my second Covid vaccination at any time and not have to wait until the pre-assessment was done, but I was not to have it on the same day as my treatment. This was music to my ears and hopefully I wouldn't have to wait too much longer. I messaged Amanda to let her know. Treatment on the 16th March went well and it was the first time I had not had the Chemotherapy.

The good news was that I didn't get my usual 'wipe out' moments a few days after treatment this time round. I actually felt quite good!!!

Viv called with my latest Blood results, and my Kidney function was still slightly raised but it was nothing to worry about. They would again repeat the Bloods in a couple of weeks and then just do a yearly check on them. I also informed her about the fact I didn't have to wait for the second Covid vaccination, and I could have it at any time apart from treatment days and she was going to look into it, and also that at last I had a telephone consultation with the Urologist on Wednesday 24th March.

On Friday 19th March, Tim and I had some great news!!! We both had a text to say that we could book our second Covid jabs!!! We wasted no time and got them booked for following Thursday. I had to go in the morning as I needed the Pfizer jab, and Tim was to go in the afternoon as he needed the Oxford AZ jab. We didn't mind this at all as we were both just so grateful to be able to get them done.

The vaccination programme, country wide, had been going exceptionally well, with daily infection rates falling and the amount of people losing their lives was dropping as well. In February the Government had put together a plan to ease us out of lock-down. This was to be that children would return to School on the 8th March, outdoor gatherings of up to six people or two households was to resume from 29th March, along with grassroots sports. Non-essential Shops, Hairdressers, Gyms and the Hospitality industry were to open on 12th April. This meant that Pubs and other food outlets could serve drinks and food but only outdoors. Two households would be able to mix indoors, with the rule of six applying to pub settings from 17th May. Legal limits on social contact were to be lifted by 21st June. I think this all made a lot of people very happy but it was all subject to change if infection rates started to rise again. Also on the 31st March shielding was to cease. Freedom!!!!!!

I took a call from Sharon on Monday 22nd March and told her I was going to try again to wean myself off the Steroids. I was on 2mg once a day and had dropped it to 1mg daily, with the view to going down to 1mg every other day and then try and stop them completely. The peeing problem was starting to get much better so I felt that now would be the time to at least try again. She also informed me that one of the other McMillan Nurses had a patient that was experiencing the same Urinary problem as me, and had been on exactly the same treatment plan, which could suggest that it may be the Chemo that was causing the problem. I found that very interesting and I did feel for the other patient.

I had a Diabetic medication review with the Doctor but he said he was more than happy for me to stay on the same tablets I was on until I had at least spoken to the Urologist. I had the telephone consultation with the Urology Consultant on Wednesday 24th March and he agreed that the next course of action would be to do the camera up the Urethra. An appointment would be made for me in the coming weeks. At last!!! We may get to the bottom of the problem.

The next day was vaccination day!!!! We had to go to a different venue for the second jab, but once again it was a well-oiled machine, with no queues, and we were in and out very quickly, and didn't feel unsafe at all. All of the Volunteers, Doctors and Nurses were brilliant. I actually felt a little emotional when I received mine, as I felt it was such an epic moment. So I was done in the morning, and Tim in the afternoon. I had the same sore arm as I had last time, and Tim had exactly the same reaction as before, being that he had mild flu like symptoms that lasted just 24 hours, and again a bath, Paracetamol and Whisky soon sorted the problem.

I had a letter come through to say that my next CT scan was booked for the 6th April, which was the same day as my next treatment. The two appointments were booked at different Hospitals, approximately 45 minutes apart. I did phone the Cancer unit to see if it was alright to have both done on the same day and they said it was fine. It was going to be a bit tight time wise, but we were sure we would manage it.

Quite unbelievably, I also had a letter to say my Cystoscopy was also booked on the 6th April!!! There was no way we were going to manage all 3 on the same day, so I phoned the Urology department and they bought the appointment forward by 1 week.

On Wednesday 31st March it was off to the Hospital again for the Cystoscopy. Now to say it was a little undignified would not be an exaggeration, but with everything I had already been through, this was going to be easy. I just had to drop my Trousers and Knickers, lay on the bed raise my knees, put my Heals together and just expose my nether region!!! So in he went!!! It was a little uncomfortable, but watching everything on the screen soon took your mind off it. Inspection done, he informed me that he could not find anything wrong with my Bladder or my Urethra. Good news in one way but it didn't explain what was going on. The obvious thing now was that it was the first round of Chemo last September that could be the main cause of the problem. It had started 3 days after that treatment, but was now getting progressively better. There now was not any other explanation.

I was now starting to sleep so much better, and was only weeing once or twice a night. It seemed to me that the Urinary problem was seriously sorting itself out, which again suggested it was the Chemo that had been causing the problem all along, as I had now been free from it for nearly six weeks.

I had my next pre-assessment on Friday 2nd April, and I mentioned to the Nurse that I had coughed up a small amount of Blood in the morning. She seemed a little concerned and she said she would call me when the Blood results came back. True to her word she did, and informed me she had spoken to someone in A&E and I was to go there to have an X-ray to rule out an infection. Off we went and three and a half hours later I finally got the results and there was no infection. Not that I minded too much, as I was just grateful that they were on the ball in case there was a problem.

Tuesday 6th April was an interesting day. We were off in the morning for the CT scan, and we were due at the other Hospital in the afternoon for my treatment. The scan went well, with the usual 'I think I've wet myself' (thankfully I didn't) liquid being used intravenously. We managed to stop at the Yummy food outlet as we realised we would make the second appointment with plenty of time to spare. Everything went well with treatment, with it again being just Immunotherapy and no Chemo.

I still felt very tired after treatment, but not the usual wipe out I was experiencing on Chemo, and it was more manageable. I was now still managing to keep up the 15 minutes on the Treadmill and Bike, with a couple of small jogs, resistance band work on my arms, and a few other exercises to help get me fitter.

I took a call from Sharon, and she seemed very encouraging when it came to me starting running again. I did explain to her that my breathing was still not great, but I would see how it went, and give it a try. The small jogs on the Treadmill were fine, but I was a little scared at that moment in time to do anymore because of my breathing. I did go and see Coach James, and he was quite helpful in as much as he said to send him records of what I was doing and how I was feeling, and he would put together a training plan for me. I could go to the track, but I was to take it very easy and probably start with some gentle Discus throws. It would be just so nice to be able to do anything as I thought at one time my Athletics time was over. I now had hope. I did pop up the track on one of their training nights, just to say hello to everyone, not to train, and the feeling of just being there put a happy bubble in my tummy. I just couldn't wait to get back.

Things were going quite well for me now. I could exercise a little more, my breathing was not so bad, and the stinging was well under control. Sleeping at night was now a pleasure, not something to be feared and I was only up on average once a night for a wee. Everyone kept banging on at me about stopping the Steroids. So I decided to give it another go. The one thing they all forgot to tell me about was the withdrawal side effects that are associated with stopping them.

I had been off them for about two weeks, and the good news was that the wee-wee problem didn't come back, but I was oh so tired, falling asleep randomly, my breathing wasn't so good, and a slight cough returned. I did have certain days where I felt semi-normal, which felt good, but that would normally be followed by tired days. Also I noticed that my sugar levels were dropping quite a lot. I got to the point that it was seriously dragging me down, so I called the Doctors and spoke to Viv. She seemed to think it could be a combination of coming off the Chemo, Steroid withdrawal and possibly my blood sugar levels being low. She spoke to one of the Doctors and it was decided that I should stop the Diabetic medication, but keep a keen eye on my sugar levels. I done what they said and my sugar levels remained within the normal range for several days, so the good news was I probably was not diabetic anymore!!!! As the Diabetes had been caused by the Steroids in the first place, it made perfect sense to me. Some good news at last.

However, I was still so tired, and my breathing was not great. Also the cough was still there but not getting any worse. I had my next pre-assessment on Friday 23rd April, and I mentioned all of this to the Nurse but she didn't really give me any advice, but made notes of it on my records.

Also on this same day, I braved going up the track for some very light training!!! All I done was walk around the track to warm up and then braved throwing the Discus. It wasn't great, but boy it felt good and I was just so glad that I was able to do it. There was a time that Tim and I thought this would never happen, but through positive thinking and determination it did! I ached a bit the next day though.

As luck had it, Sharon called me on Monday 27th April and I explained all of my problems to her. She checked my blood results and they were fine and she looked at the last CT scan report and she told me that the Tumour was still stable. There was no obvious reason for my latest complications. I was due for my next round of treatment on the Tuesday so she agreed to come and see me in person, and stated that she would probably need to get in touch with Dr Cominos. I was just hoping and praying they didn't suggest going back on the Steroids. I had worked so hard on weaning myself off them that the thought of that made me shudder!!!! True to her word, she did come to see me whilst I was waiting to go in for my treatment, and she was still at a loss as to why I was feeling so rough sometimes. She advised me to give it another week and she would call me again. Any problems in the meantime I was to call her. The treatment went well as usual.

BACK ON TRACK!!!

For the next three days, for some unknown reason, I felt the best I had in weeks!!!! Either it was all of the side effects wearing off, or something else going on I didn't know, but I was just so grateful to be feeling good. I could exercise a bit more, and even braved the track again on the Friday evening, with a walk round the track, some Discus throws, which were better than last week, and some very small hurdle walk overs which Coach James had suggested I did. On the Saturday I had felt good again up until about 5pm when I noticed my chest was a little crackly. I started to cough a fair bit and what happened next took us both by surprise. I coughed up the most hideous amount of blood with clots in it, and every time I coughed it just kept coming. It was like something out of a vampire horror movie. We were both very concerned, and Tim dialled 111 straight away and they advised us to go straight to A&E and that they had made us an appointment for 5.30pm and that I needed to be seen within the hour. So off we went and was met by a Nurse who told us to book in. We were then told to go to an Urgent Care Unit to be seen. As luck had it Tim was allowed to come in with me. We booked in and then waited. And waited, and waited. It got to about 6.30pm and Tim asked the Receptionist what was happening as we were told that I needed to be seen within the hour, only to be told the hour started when we saw the Nurse at A&E. So we waited some more, and eventually we saw a Doctor at about 6.50pm. She asked a lot of questions and then told us to go back to A&E!!!!! So much for the hour. Back we went and this time Tim could not come in with me. I had my Bloods taken, and then I was put in a side room for my own protection against Covid. At 9pm I still had not seen anyone so I went to the reception desk which was manned by some lovely Nurses and explained I had been waiting for three and a half hours, and when they looked on the system it said I had only been waiting for two hours. They explained that the waiting time re-started the second time I booked in at A&E. I was not impressed. I asked them about being seen within one hour as was explained by 111, only to be told that 111 tell everyone the same!!!!! It got to about 10pm and I was starting to feel very anxious, tired and very hungry as

I had not eaten since 2pm that afternoon. A lovely Nurse was kind enough to bring me a sandwich and a coffee, and I tried to explain how I was feeling and that I would give it another half an hour and I was going home.

She said she would chase things up for me. It got to 10.30pm and that was it for me. I was out of there. I went to one of the Nurses and asked them to remove the Cannula as I was going home, and she politely asked me to give her five minutes to chase up the Doctor. Lo and behold, five minutes later the Doctor appeared. She sent me for an X-ray and as luck had it she was still there when I arrived back in my room. She explained that the coughing up of the blood was quite normal (not in my book it wasn't) and that I had a cavity in my chest so it was probably just a build-up of mucous and blood, and that there was really nothing to worry about. Easy for her to say!!!! My bloods were all fine and nothing showed up on the X-ray so she was happy to send me home, and advised me to start on a course of anti-biotics which I had at home. I was always led to believe, and was told by many during this journey, that if you didn't have a temperature, you didn't have an infection. I asked the Doctor about this, and she said you can get an infection without having a temperature. She also advised me to listen to my body, and if I suspected anything was wrong then just to take a course. I was discharged at approximately 11.30pm. The whole episode from phone call to finish had taken six and a half hours. But I was glad to be home and I was grateful that nothing serious was going on.

Quite frankly, it was obvious that the system was broken, and it was the poor Nurses that were bearing the brunt of this. One of the Nurses explained to me that the day before, she had been verbally abused by a lot of patients who had been waiting for ages. This is just so unfair on them, as they are just doing their job, and are not responsible for decisions made regarding systems. Someone really does need to have a look at this, even if it's just for the safety of the lovely Nurses.

Consequently, because of Saturday, I was completely wiped out Sunday and Monday and couldn't do anything but sleep. On the Tuesday I felt really good again, and managed some exercise. Sharon called as she was concerned as she had heard what had happened, and she also re-iterated that it was quite normal to cough up a large amount of blood, and that she knew of many patients who had done the same. If only I had known.

For the next week or so things seemed to calm down a lot. I now knew I wasn't Diabetic anymore, my breathing was getting easier and my fatigue seemed to have abated a lot. I found myself with a lot more energy, and was not feeling tired all the time. I still felt a bit weary on occasions, but nothing like I was experiencing before. I was managing more exercise at home, and had encountered another track training session which went really well.

On Saturday 8th May, I had to have another Ultrasound Scan of my abdomen at the Hospital, which had been requested by the Doctors, but thankfully it showed up nothing new. I think the Doctors had requested it in response to the wee-wee problem, but by now that was nowhere near as bad as it had been, and we had established that it most likely had been caused by the Chemotherapy.

Thursday 13th May, we had another review appointment with Dr Cominos the Oncologist, and the news was great again. The tumour was stable and had not grown, and had again not spread anywhere else!!!! This again was music to our ears. We also asked her some questions mainly relating to returning to work. Tim was still working from home, but we both knew at some point he would have to return to site, albeit on fleeting visits, with the bulk of his work still being done from home. She said it was fine for him to return, but still be careful. I asked about returning also, but she said that decision was up to me, and I would have to judge it depending on how I felt. It was something I was going to have to give a lot of thought to, as I was still unsure about returning. Part of me wanted to, but part of me was concerned about letting my work colleagues down if I didn't feel up to it on certain days. I was going to have to contemplate this one long and hard and make a decision at some point. We also asked her about my training, and she seemed to think it was a good idea and would help with my breathing. She did explain that I couldn't do any harm to the tumour, but again said I just had to listen to my body. This again was good news to me as I had been a bit apprehensive about pushing too hard in case I done some irreversible damage. I now knew I could push a little harder. Within reason of course.

On the Friday I attended another training session at the track, and it was the best one yet!!! Managed a 400m walk around the track, with three small jogs, done the warm up drills, jogged 10m with a walk back followed by a jog to 20m with walk back and done the same to 30m!!!! I managed to do this three times and pushed a little harder on the third run through and it felt amazing!!!! I also threw some really good Discus and Shot Put. It felt so good to be back on track.

FINAL THOUGHTS.

So, This is where I am so far on my Journey, and I'm sure you will agree so far it's been one hell of a ride!!! I don't know how long this journey will go on for, no-body does, but it's not the end, or the beginning of the end, but the end of the beginning. For the best part I have stayed strong and positive, despite a few little wobbles, and I intend to stay that way for as long as possible.

At the beginning of this journey I had kept a daily journal. Every day I would write in it what had happened, good or bad, and how I was feeling. It wasn't easy at first, like everything that is new, but once I got into the routine of doing it, it became easy. I would strongly recommend to anyone finding themselves in the same situation as myself to do this, and to be frank and honest when doing so. It always helps to write things down on paper, and you have a permanent record of goings on, either good or bad. Should you be someone who is acquainted to anybody on a similar journey, I would urge you to recommend to them to keep a daily journal. It was reading back through my journal that inspired me to write this book.

It was actually when I started writing this book, that I realised this experience was not personal to me, but there could be others out there going through the same, if not worse. I realised that maybe, just maybe, I could help someone with some of the feelings and encounters I had experienced, and boy there were a lot of them.

I learned very quickly that you have to learn how to paddle your own Canoe sometimes, and become an absolute pain in the 'butt'!!!!! There are answers out there to your questions, but sometimes you really have to 'kick ass' to get them. Don't be frightened to ask questions. On several occasions I didn't and then regretted it afterwards.

Another thing that really helps is writing lists of questions, and leaving space for the answers. When you are put in a difficult situation, the brain can sometimes go numb, and it's not until later on you think of all the questions you wanted to ask. This happened to me on several occasions, and then I learned the art of list writing. This helped immensely, and again I would highly recommenced it. Don't be frightened to ask anything. In my mind there is no such thing as a dumb question. It may be important to you and that's all that matters. If you are lucky enough to have someone that can support you, or you can support someone on their journey, make lists a priority when dealing with people either face to face, or on the phone. If you find that you have to deal with things on your own, then, possibly ask the Macmillan Nurses or someone from the Hospice to help. If they can't, they will point you in the right direction to get the help you may need. There is a lot of help out there, but again you do have to ask, but it's worth it in the end.

As you can tell, along the journey there has been some up and down times. The down times are the ones to watch. They can take over your mind and quite frankly make you feel anxious, frustrated and stressed, amongst many feelings you may encounter. These are not good feelings and can cause other problems. You may say it was easy for me because I have a 'Tim'. I admit, he is my rock, and has seen me through some very dark times, but I am the one in control of my mind, and when I have felt low or down, that's when I know I have to control it myself. Mindfulness really helps and there are a lot of websites out there that can guide you in the right direction with this. Also, having a good Mind-set, a Positive Attitude, and maintaining a sense of Humour really helps!!!!

I have never at any point been in denial of the Cancer, but I have denied it taking over my life. I know it's there, but when it comes into my head I use what is called a 'Shifter' to get it out. A Shifter can be anything. Your favourite food, your favourite Holiday, or just anything that puts a smile on your face. You cannot feel down and smile at the same time!!! So smile more!!!!!!

So summing up, keep a journal, write questions down, be a pain in the 'butt' and smile more!!!!!!

Another reason I decided to write this book, was to try and raise funds for Charity. I sadly could not climb mountains or run marathons. At one point I couldn't even climb up the stairs!!! I wanted to do something, so I guessed a book would be a good idea. I have decided that all profits from this book should be evenly split between, Cancer research, Macmillan Nurses, and the local Hospice. I could not decide on just one of them so went for all three. These are all more or less self-funding, and at the moment need all the help they can get. I also couldn't choose just one as they are all so amazing. Without the research, cures cannot be found. The care and dedication of the Nurses is second to none, and the Hospice is there to help when you need it.

I really need to say thank you to some very special people.

Obviously, thank you Tim for everything.

Also a huge thank you to my Dad and Audrey, Derek my Brother and Jackie his wife, and Lorain my little Sister, for all of the support and love that you extended to me during my Journey.

To all at Thanet Athletics Club, especially James my Coach, who was always there for me; To all of my work colleagues especially Tineka the Boss and Lyn my Reception buddy for your constant updates on work, and the socially distanced hugs!!!! To my neighbours who never waned in their care and compassion, and their constant supply of flowers, chocolate and grapes!!!!! And basically anyone else who knows me.

Also I need to extend a huge thank you to all of the healthcare workers and Doctors who helped to look after me when I needed it. This also includes assistants, domestic workers, and anyone else employed by the NHS. Given the unprecedented times we have faced, they have all gone above and beyond their duties to give myself, and anyone else who has needed their care, the utmost professionalism and understanding.

I would like to also extend a thank you to *YOU*, my dear reader, for coming with me on my journey. I sincerely hope you never find yourself in a situation where you have to start your own journey, but if you do, maybe some of what I have experienced and learnt along the way may help.

In Athletics terms, I have learnt that life is not a sprint, but a wonderful Marathon that should be enjoyed, not endured. Very often we take everything for granted, until we are forced to take a look at just how lucky we are with what we already have around us.

So for now, Take *your* marks…….. Get set…………. And enjoy this wonderful Marathon called life.

May you be happy, May you be Strong, May you be protected, always.

Lyn. X

Lightning Source UK Ltd.
Milton Keynes UK
UKHW012318100921
390336UK00001B/36